Editorial

*S*UCH IS THE power of recording that companies can now, more than ever before, actually 'create' an artist's career. The fact that making a name for oneself is no longer entirely dependent on long and arduous tours around the globe (though of course concert-giving remains an essential part of the equation) has meant that artists can rise to fame much more easily – and rapidly. The young Russian pianist Arcadi Volodos is a case in point. Sony Classical signed him in 1995, when few people outside the pianophile world had heard of him, and there was then a period of about a year when the two sides negotiated the repertoire that was to be on his first disc, which was recorded in 1996 and released the following year. Volodos's concerto début in the UK took place when he played Rach 2 at the Proms with Riccardo Chailly. The notices were good, as they had been for his Wigmore Hall solo début, but it was only when Sony released his disc of transcriptions a few months later that he suddenly became big news. Here, for all the world to see, was an enormous talent, a remarkably mature-looking and sounding 25-year-old with a perfect balance of musicianship and technique.

Having a success of that magnitude is one thing, sustaining it is quite another. Sony has followed up the first disc with a recording derived from Volodos's Carnegie Hall début. It claims to be live, which is not entirely true – though more as a result of audience noise than pianistic fallibility (a subject that is considered by Michael Glover in 'Pianophilia' on page 112) – but by any standards it is a considerable achievement. Those Beckmessers who complained that the repertoire on the first disc wasn't of sufficient substance to be able to judge his playing will find the second disc only slightly more engaging. The point is not whether or not Volodos *can* interpret a Beethoven sonata effectively, or whether he has a feel for Chopin *mazurkas*, but whether he has something significant to say in his chosen repertoire. Just because he's not proving easy to pigeon-hole should not be an excuse for cheap jibes.

Interestingly, Volodos's recent London recital (a near match of New York in terms of repertoire) was greeted with widespread scepticism from the daily press. If the recital itself didn't quite attain the dizzy heights of New York, it was nevertheless still extraordinary by most standards, making the dichotomy between what was heard and what was written all the more inexplicable. Could it be that the press, tired of record-company hype, were making a statement – consciously or otherwise – more driven by politics than music? It will be fascinating to follow Volodos in the coming years, to see how his playing develops and changes, and in what directions his repertoire expands.

Publicity, subtly handled, can be a powerful tool. In 1955, when Columbia Records released for the first time ever, part of Hofmann's fabled 1937 Golden Jubilee Concert, it was greeted with great public and critical adulation in spite of the fact, as Gregor Benko points out in his appraisal of Hofmann's recorded legacy on page 12, it was 'sonically substandard even for the time'. Substandard or not, it was still precious for enshrining on record one of the great concerts in piano history. Perhaps future generations will come to regard Volodos's Carnegie Hall début in a similar light – as the memento of a great occasion. **Harriet Smith**

Editor	**Harriet Smith**
Consulting Editors	**Donald Manildi**
	Bryce Morrison
	Michael Spring
Editorial Consultant	**Michael Glover**
Production Editor	**Emma Roach**
Assistant Production Editor	**Katherine Bettley**
Sub-editor	**Nick Flower**
Advertisement Manager	**Paul Geoghegan**
Production Controller	**Jo Frost**
Subscription Manager	**Jenny Savage**
Circulation Manager	**Nick Clements**
Marketing Manager	**Verity Batchelder**
Production Manager	**Dermot Jones**
Designer	**Mark Jubber**
Editorial Director	**Christopher Pollard**
Publisher	**Anthony Pollard**

Volume 2 · Number 7

Front cover Arcadi Volodos
Photo courtesy Lebrecht Collection/Mares

International Piano Quarterly is published quarterly. US Subscription price is $38·00. Periodicals postage paid at Rahway NJ. US Postmaster please send address corrections to *IPQ*, c/o Mercury Airfreight International Ltd, 2323 Randolph Avenue, Avenel, New Jersey NJ 07001.

Published by Gramophone Publications Limited
135 Greenford Road, Sudbury Hill, Harrow,
Middlesex HA1 3YD, Great Britain
Telephone +44 (0)181-422 4562
Fax +44 (0)181-869 8400

A pianistic idol: Josef Hofmann. Page 12

Photo courtesy Gregor Benko

Contents

The art of self-criticism: Piotr Anderszewski. Page 30

Photo Noelle

Eileen Joyce: all work and no play. Page 34

Photo courtesy Bryce Morrison

Ravel's Left-Hand Concerto on record. Page 38 *Photo AKG, London*

Hidden talent:
Ignace
Tiegerman.
Page 54
*Photo courtesy
Allan Evans*

Leon Fleisher in
conversation:
Page 58 *Photo
ICM
Artists/Steiner*

Living up to
expectations:
Arcadi Volodos.
Page 64 *Photo
Sony Classical*

The next issue will be published on July 5th, 1999

In the next issue ...

- A collector's guide to Chopin's *Etudes*

- Dinu Lipatti remembered by Mark Ainley

- David Fanning examines the Polish piano tradition

International Piano Quarterly is published in the spring (April), summer (July),
autumn (October) and winter (January). *IPQ* is available through specialist
record dealers and on postal subscription. For subscription details see page
108. While every effort has been made to ensure the accuracy of statements in
this magazine, we cannot accept responsibility for any errors or omissions, or
for matters arising from clerical or printers' errors, or for an advertiser not
completing his contract.
Printed in England by Cradley Print Limited ISSN 1368-9770

Key to symbols

	Compact Disc
	Compact Cassette
	Long Playing Record
	78rpm Record
	VHS
	LaserDisc
⒡	Full price £10 and over
ⓜ	Medium price £7 – £9·99
ⓑ	Bargain price £5 – £6·99

Abbreviated dates in brackets denote original
review dates in *Gramophone* (A/97 denotes the
Awards issue). *IPQ* review dates, where applicable,
follow *Gramophone* dates and are indicated as
follows: Sp (Spring issue); Su (Summer);
A (Autumn); W (Winter), together with the
year in which the review was published. Reissues
are listed as ^R; when a date appears as, say,
7/56^R it means the recording was first reviewed
in July 1956 but has since been reissued under
the listed number, though not re-reviewed.

Letters

Letters should be sent to
**The Editor, International Piano Quarterly,
135 Greenford Road, Sudbury Hill, Harrow,
Middlesex HA1 3YD, Great Britain**
E-mail ipq@gramophone.co.uk

The Editor does not necessarily agree with any views expressed in
letters printed, and reserves the right to edit correspondence
where necessary.

Restoration or devastation?

Apropos Mr Patterson's letter in the Summer
issue of *IPQ*, there is surely no topic more likely
to cause argument and dissension among
collectors than the method of transferring
historic material to CD. Does one go for the
natural non-interventionist approach, apply
computer processing to remove all vestiges of
surface hiss and crackle, or perhaps follow an
intermediate route using relatively light selective
filtering? Personally I would consign CEDAR
equipment and its ilk to the nearest skip and
advocate a generally non-interventionist stance.
From my listening experience it is just not
possible to apply computer-processing
technology without destroying the presence,
immediacy and ambience, leaving the recording
sounding dull, dead and lifeless (not adequately
remedied by then adding artificial reverberation).
I actually find some 78rpm piano recordings
more natural than those modern digital masters
made with such tremendous reverberation that
they sound as if recorded in a cavern.

Perhaps it's coincidental, but out of many
historic CDs in my collection, principally
piano, my favourite recordings all have natural
transfers, as if one were hearing the original
recordings. Indeed, on one occasion, shortly
after purchasing a CD player, I was so moved
at seemingly hearing one of my favourite 78s
again, after a gap of many years, that I actually
started out of my chair in readiness to turn it
over for the expected side-break!

In my opinion, the best piano transfers have
appeared from Colin Attwell and Denis Hall
on Pearl. Yes, they have high surface hiss, but
they also sound completely natural, with the
full acoustic presence and liveliness of the
originals. Four of these Pearl and Opal discs
(one anonymously transferred) stand head and
shoulders above all other piano CD reissues
that I have heard, artistically, musically and
from the standpoint of the transfers, too. These
are: an Irene Scharrer disc (Pearl ①
GEMMCD9978, 7/94), an Eileen Joyce recital
(Pearl ① GEMMCD9022, 2/94), Fanny Davies
in Schumann (Pearl ① GEMMCD9291) and
'Pupils of Leschetizky' (Opal ① CD9839, 4/89).
This latter disc contains two of the most
exquisitely beautiful piano recordings I have
ever heard: Mark Hambourg's Gluck/Sgambati
Orfeo excerpt and a Rameau Gavotte played by
Marie Novello. The disc also includes Ignaz
Friedman's incomparable Chopin *Nocturne*,
Op. 55 No. 2. Quite beyond superlatives.

Nicholas Dodson Coleman, Merseyside

Liszt's alter ego?

I much enjoyed the 'Collector's Guide' to
Liszt's B minor Sonata in the Winter issue. I
also much enjoy a good deal about Henry
Litolff; however, since he neither recorded
Liszt's music nor, to the best of my knowledge,
actually composed any of it, I would be
interested to know why he (I think?) is trying to
pass himself off photographically as his senior
colleague on page 2? He may have done more
than enough to qualify in the philandering
department, but, musical considerations aside,
'warts and all' have dwindled to no warts at all,
as your picture makes full-frontally clear.
Impressive bags under the eyes are surely no
substitute. Were these two gents side by side in
some old Scholes rogues' gallery, I wonder?

Francis Pott, Oxford

[Well spotted! Our apologies to all parties – *Ed.*]

A sound choice for some

I'm a lot more enthusiastic about Philips's
Great Pianists of the 20th Century than Alan
Thorpe Albeson appears to be in the Winter

issue of *IPQ*. While those with very large record/CD collections may find this series offers little new, I expect there are many like me with a modest collection of recordings, mostly by big names of the present day, who will find lots of new and unexpected things in the Philips project.

I feel this series has got a lot going for it. The albums are reasonably priced and provide a good cross-section of each pianist's style and technique, with informative biographical and artistic information. The packaging is very attractive, too, with the book format and the stylish covers featuring bits of a Steinway Model D, that will surely delight any lover of pianists and piano music.

I do agree with Mr Albeson that the provision of additional CDs for some artists seems a bit arbitrary, and makes one wonder what the mission is for this series; I would have preferred just a double album for each pianist (with details of additional available recordings), and a few more pianists added to the list along the lines suggested by Mr Albeson.

That said, I'm looking forward to future issues in the series and hope Philips will make the series available for a long time so that one can gradually collect and appreciate this wealth of recorded piano music.

Hugh Walker, Dunfermline, Scotland

The 'virtual' truth

As well as being a recent and enthusiastic reader of *IPQ*, I am also a regular reader of, and contributor to, an internet newsgroup which has recently entertained some lively discussions regarding the Great Pianists of the 20th Century series on Philips. To get a feeling for the consensus of our newsgroup, I recently conducted a poll, requesting that newsgroup members cast votes in the following three categories: 'Top Ten' (if you were in charge of the Philips project, but were limited to only ten pianists, who would they be?); the 'Ten Most Neglected' (who would you have included in this collection that Philips did not select?); and the 'Ten Most Overrated' (of the pianists selected by Philips, who would you have omitted in favour of more deserving pianists?).

I received 475 votes from participants in the UK, USA, Canada, Germany, The Netherlands, and Chile, and thought that your readers might be interested in the results:

Top Ten
(1) Richter; (2) Rachmaninov; (3) Hofmann; (4-5 tied) Cortot; (4-5 tied) Horowitz; (6) Schnabel; (7-10 tied) Friedman; (7-10 tied) Lipatti; (7-10 tied) Rubinstein; (7-10 tied) Sofronitsky.

Neglected
(1) Petri; (2) Nat; (3) Busoni; (4) Barere; (5-6 tied) Ciani; (5-6 tied) Sokolov; (7-10 tied) Egorov; (7-10 tied) Feinberg; (7-10 tied) Rosenthal; (7-10 tied) Zhukov.

Overrated
(1) Previn; (2) Uchida; (3) Schiff; (4) Watts; (5) Haebler; (6-9 tied) Eschenbach; (6-9 tied) Gieseking; (6-9 tied) Kissin; (6-9 tied) Pires; (10-19 tied) Anda; (10-19 tied) Argerich; (10-19 tied) Ashkenazy; (10-19 tied) Barenboim; (10-19 tied) Van Cliburn; (10-19 tied) Curzon; (10-19 tied) Gould; (10-19 tied) Janis; (10-19 tied) Pollini (10-19 tied); Wild (10-19 tied).

I felt compelled to award a special prize to Walter Gieseking as 'Most Controversial Pianist' since he garnered a place in the 'Overrated' list, but also missed the 'Top Ten' ranking by only a single vote.

Jeremy Cook, Connecticut, USA

Discographical giants

I am grateful to Donald Manildi for pointing out, in your Winter 1999 issue (page 78), some of the errors in my volume of discographies *More Giants of the Keyboard*.

As Mr Manildi must know, there is no such thing as a definitive discography, because reissues of familiar material are constantly reaching the record lists and because, in our historically aware age, new discoveries are even being made in areas which we might have assumed to be exhausted. From one reader, I recently received advice – which I am now investigating – that certain of Rubinstein's post-war Chopin recordings were made not in New York, as I had stated, nor in Hollywood, as Mr Manildi asserts, but in Rome!

Concerning catalogue numbers, I endeavour to list as many as possible of those applicable to major territories of issue. In the cases of Horowitz and Rubinstein, I would certainly be glad to have from Mr Manildi details of the important American issue numbers which he maintains are absent from my discography. The same applies to the mono LP numbers which he claims are 'masquerading' as stereo ones.

My brief is to provide a guide for the general, or shall we say amateur, collector of old recordings, and to ensure that the data is presented in a user-friendly manner which is comprehensible to those who do not possess qualifications in librarianship. Hence my decision, among others, to adopt a lower-case style for the headings of composers' individual works: this is a recognized design device which provides visual relief in a layout which inevitably involves much repetition. Opus numbers are provided when they are necessary to distinguish single works within a group, but not when the group, such as the Chopin *Préludes*, for example, has one overall number. When dealing with performers from the gramophone's past, I feel it justifiable to retain the numbering systems which were applicable at the time, hence the Longo numbers for Scarlatti – these are the numbers which appear on the old editions sought by collectors.

While appreciating Mr Manildi's criticisms, which are constructive, I fail to understand why I should be discouraged from providing a useful service at a realistic price.

John Hunt, London

And in reply ...

Mr Hunt's notion that a bad job serves a purpose for those who know no better merely reinforces the serious concerns expressed in my review. It is precisely those users of his book who are *not* expert in the field who will be most easily misled by his errors. Neither I nor anyone else insists on a 'definitive' discography, but it is not unreasonable to expect certain minimum standards of accuracy to be met. It is nice to know that Mr Hunt is 'glad to have details' from me, but the time to seek help is before, not after, publication.

Concerning Rubinstein, his solo recordings from 1947 to the mid-1950s were made in Hollywood, as I stated. The RCA Italiana studios in Rome did not open until 1963, and Rubinstein's first recording there was his stereo version of the Chopin *Waltzes*. Mr Hunt, however, persists in identifying these and all of Rubinstein's Italian sessions as originating in New York. Again, the correct information should have been determined before publication.

I might also observe that Mr Hunt's use of lower-case titles is a recent development that is not present in his earlier volume of pianists nor in the majority of his other publications.

Under the circumstances, given the unreliability of his work, Mr Hunt's description of his discographies as 'user-friendly' is hard to take seriously. Until he chooses to expend the necessary effort to improve his publications, he will continue to do a disservice to his users, to the musicians whose recordings he purports to document, and to his own reputation.

Donald Manildi, Maryland, USA

The pianist and the mayfly

Has anybody ever noticed the connection between 'dying young and beautiful' and the common pianist? Flicking through the pages of my *IPQ*, how often I find a pianist's name followed by the morbid statement 'killed in a plane crash' or 'died aged just 22'. I have sometimes wondered if there isn't some bizarre piano festival being assembled in heaven; the number of pianists who meet untimely deaths does seem unusually high. Just a few who spring to mind are Dino Ciani (1941-74), William Kapell (1922-53), killed in a plane crash on his way back from Australia, Noel Mewton-Wood (1922-53), Dinu Lipatti (1917-50), Yuri Egorov (1954-88), Terence Judd (1957-79), Julius Katchen (1926-69), Steven de Groote (1953-89), Marc Raubenheimer (1952-84), Mischa Levitzki (1898-1941) ... Is this a coincidence or 'should we be told'?

Gordon Dobie, Istanbul, Turkey

A writer's request

I wonder if anyone has biographical information concerning Eleanor Donaldson, who was a prominent British concert pianist in the 1930s and 1940s. She was married to a Scottish Presbyterian minister, the Reverend R. D. Menzies. I am also interested in pursuing news of their son Hamish Menzies, who emigrated to America in the 1950s and who was a pianist and composer, albeit in a lighter vein. Any information about his family would be most gratefully appreciated by this writer who is alas, not as 'well up' on the world of classical music as I would wish.

Raymond Smith, Canada

Now there's no need to choose between a digital piano and a real one.

*A*ll the natural beauty and tone of a real piano. All the convenience and control of a digital one. Sounds too good to be true?

Meet The Silent Piano from Yamaha.

First of all it's a genuine Yamaha piano. Upright or grand.

But activate the unique Silent System™ and an ingenious damping mechanism silences the strings and instead, the sound comes from Yamaha's brilliant digital piano tone generator.

The transition is seamless. The touch doesn't change.

But silent practice on headphones means neighbours and family are undisturbed.

You'll need to know more. So for a free information pack, call 01908 369238 today.

Yamaha-Kemble Music (UK) Ltd. Acoustic Division, Sherbourne Drive, Tilbrook, Milton Keynes MK7 8BL
E-mail: acoustic_sales@infomta.post.yamaha.co.jp
www.yamaha.co.jp/english/product/piano/

YAMAHA PIANO
Silent
SERIES

'Transfer' heaven

Look out for some exciting releases coming soon from APR: in spring it will bring out the complete 1947 recordings of Dinu Lipatti, released together for the first time. The disc includes the first ever CD transfer of Lipatti's *first* recording of 'Jesu, joy of man's desiring'. And following on from its highly regarded first disc of Medtner playing Medtner (reviewed A/98), comes a second volume. Also released this spring is an all-Beethoven recital by Benno Moiseiwitsch which includes two previously unreleased takes. More historic reissues are also due from Arbiter, with the release in June of Samuel Feinberg's 'Berlin and Moscow recordings, 1929-1948', containing works by Bach, Bach/Feinberg, Schumann, Liszt, Liadov and Scriabin.

Chopin celebrations

In honour of the 150th anniversary of the death of Chopin, Krystian Zimerman will be undertaking an extensive tour, performing the two concertos (directed from the keyboard) in some 28 different venues. Commencing in Bologna on August 15th, he will travel through Italy, Austria, Poland Germany, Belgium, France, Britain, Holland, Switzerland and America. His final performance will be a second concert in Warsaw on November 19th, after which he will presumably be ready for a change of repertoire! A recording of the concertos will be released by DG in the late autumn.

Opus 111 will be approaching Chopin's anniversary from a slightly different angle, bringing out a set of six CDs celebrating Chopin's life and times. The first volume will feature a Polish ensemble performing some of the traditional dances that influenced Chopin's musical language, and a recital played on the composer's own piano. Later volumes will include a re-creation of Chopin's last concert in Warsaw, the reissue of Grigory Sokolov's *Preludes, Etudes*, Op. 25, and Second Sonata, and a disc of excerpts from letters by Chopin and George Sand recited in French with musical interludes. The final volume will feature jazz transcriptions of various Chopin works!

Festive Rachmaninov

London's first ever Rachmaninov festival will take place at the South Bank from May 6th-23rd, and will feature an impressive roster of Russian artists, including **Arcadi Volodos** in Rachmaninov's Third Piano Concerto on the 11th and **Mikhail Pletnev** performing the *Paganini* Rhapsody on the 16th, both with the Philharmonia Orchestra conducted by Vladimir Ashkenazy, **Evgeni Kissin** will be tackling an all-Russian programme which will include the *Etudes-tableaux*, Op. 39, Scriabin's Third Sonata and Balakirev's *Islamey* on the 17th and, on the 23rd, a duo recital by **Nikolai Demidenko** and **Dmitri Alexeev** will include Rachmaninov's Second Suite, Op.17.

The festival will also feature the first screening, on May 9th, of a major new documentary film about the composer, its central theme relating the desperate journey Rachmaninov and his family made on Christmas Eve, 1917, to escape the backlash of the October Revolution. The exceptional archive footage was supplied by the composer's grandson, who will also be reminiscing in person about his grandfather during the course of the festival. There will also be a video release of the film from NVC Arts to coincide with the South Bank Festival (telephone 0171-960 4242).

Great Expectations

Once there was the famous adversarial encounter between Mozart and Clementi, and then the even more notorious Liszt-Thalberg play-off some 50 years later. Nowadays, it seems from the proliferation of such contests as though a gladiatorial army travels the world month after month in the hope, if only by attrition, of winning a moment of ephemeral glory. These dragons' teeth, once sown, carry the potential not only for their own destruction, but also of a far wider and longer-term debasement of an essentially expressive medium. Moreover, it is a medium whose constituent elements do not lend themselves at all readily to the type of objective appraisal necessary, at any but the most basic level, for any such occasion to maintain whatever credibility it may aspire to. *Cui bono?* But then, as Miss Jean Brodie might have said, 'If that's the sort of thing you like ... .'

A cursory glance through the programme-booklet of the Concorso Pianistico Internationale 'Premio Franco Durante', held November 25th-29th last year in Frattamaggiore, highlights the nature and extent of the problem. Some 50 pianists, ranging in age from 16-35, from across the world (as well as from Italy!), many with impressive lists of prizes already in their portfolios (Calgary, Bolzano, Paris, 'Dino Ciani' and so on), had foregathered on the outskirts of Naples to convince an august panel of jurors that they were possessed of the necessary qualities not only to fulfil a list of engagements in Italy and Belgium but also to sustain a career after the hubbub had died down, or at least until the next competition winners were snapping at their heels!

From the lists of referees and teachers attributed to the aspirants, which read like a veritable *Who's Who* of the piano world, the degree of excellence should have been remarkable, if such endorsements are to be taken at face value. The same expectations might also have been raised by the programmes chosen, many of which, if unsurprising in content, were, nevertheless, highly demanding. In the event, however, there was an all-too-predictable desperation about much of the playing, especially in the case of some of the older artists, for whom the event seemed to represent a kind of 'Custer's Last Stand', while the technical vulnerability of some of the other competitors proved an insurmountable obstacle to any real communicative powers they may or may not have had.

It would be wrong, of course, to suggest that all the performances were so marred by the added pressures of the circumstances. Oliver Kern, the eventual Third Prize-winner, for example, made enough of an impression in the Berg Sonata and the Brahms *Ballades*, Op. 10, to raise one's hopes, only to disappoint in the Beethoven First Concerto in the final round. Equally, the First Prize-winner, Giuseppe Andaloro – one of the youngest entrants – seemed, perhaps understandably, to promise more for the future in the Beethoven Fourth Concerto than he actually delivered on this occasion, begging the question of the appropriateness of the concert exposure that comes with such trophies.

Concurrent with the competition, an 'Omaggio a Sergio Fiorentino' took place at the Galleria Principe in Naples – Fiorentino was to have been President of the Jury at Frattamaggiore, his administrative duties ably taken over by his former student, Mario Coppola. The contrast between the two events could hardly have been greater. An exhibition of memorabilia and a symposium in the presence of Signora Magdalena Fiorentino, at which fulsome tributes were paid by friends and colleagues, were each as moving as the examples of Fiorentino's artistry heard on this occasion. If only the spirit of Fiorentino's dictum: 'Forget everything – there is only you and the piano' could have been more evident at the competition ... there must be another way. Would that it could be found! **Charles Hopkins**

The art of video

Following on from the 'Art of Singing' and the 'Art of Conducting' NVC Arts will be releasing an 'Art of Piano' in the autumn. The video will include rare archive footage of such keyboard luminaries as Rubinstein, Horowitz and Gilels, the latter, a propaganda film showing Gilels performing Rachmaninov's *Prelude* in G minor, Op. 23 No. 6, to the Russian air force in the middle of a field in 1943! The release will also feature extensive interviews with various international artists of today, including Evgeni Kissin and Zoltán Kocsis.

The finest Godowsky Studies you've *never* heard ...?

Godowsky enthusiasts have been excitedly exchanging copies of a recently-surfaced amateur videotape of Italian pianist Francesco Libetta playing the complete *Studies on Chopin Etudes* at two concerts in Milan in 1994 and 1995. Libetta masters the technical difficulties with such confidence that he is able to imbue the works with all those attributes – poetry, drama, fire and real heart – that so many other pianists miss out in their struggle just to get round the notes. Godowsky biographer, Jeremy Nicholas, has declared them: 'Stunning. I never thought I'd hear such mesmerizing performances of these pieces in concert.'

Now 30, Libetta – who studied composition and orchestration in Paris, and philosophy and law in Italy – first performed the 53 Godowsky *Studies* in 1990 (after which his career was interrupted by military service) and would now like to make a commercial recording of the complete cycle, ideally a video or DVD release of live concert performances. Libetta is resolute in his opinion that the best case can be made for the *Studies* via recitals of substantial portions or the entire set: 'I don't like to play in recital only a few *Studies*. The visionary aspect of performing the whole corpus is important, because the texture of the *Studies* – being composed not of a muscular but of a "counterpointistic" and thus "cerebral" virtuosity – is very often not sufficiently potent (like Rachmaninov) or witty (like Friedman) to make the pieces individually appealing for the 'secular' concert-going public. As a result, there is the risk of people who do not understand the purpose of Godowsky's work concluding, "Oh, but I prefer the original Chopin".' For this reason, Libetta has never mixed the original Chopin and Godowsky's reworkings in a single concert, although he is interested in the idea of performing the Chopin on a period Pleyel, followed by the Godowsky on a modern Steinway, 'in order to demonstrate the development in technique, both in piano construction and writing.' The pianist whom Aldo Ciccolini described in 1988 as 'the most gifted artist of his generation' has also performed Ligeti and Alkan *Studies*, a cycle of all 32 Beethoven sonatas, and has recorded for the Promusica and Agora labels; future recording projects may include discs of Strauss/Godowsky and Beethoven's *Diabelli Variations*. This year will see Libetta playing Chopin's complete *oeuvre* for piano, and working on a planned recital of all of Horowitz's transcriptions. He is also interested in a repeat of Godowsky's historic Berlin début, where the great pianist-transcriber performed Brahms's First Concerto, seven of his *Studies*, his arrangement of Weber's *Invitation to the Dance* and then (as a gloriously rich dessert) the Tchaikovsky First. Amidst such furious pianistic activity, Libetta has also found time for conducting and composing – his three-act opera *Iopa* is still in progress, but parts have been performed at the Villa Medici in Rome, Lecce and Catania, whilst extended symphonic excerpts will be premièred by the Bari Sympony Orchestra this September. **IPQ**

Francesco Libetta: 'the most gifted pianist of his generation'?
Photo Donetti

A VERY FRENCH PIANIST

JEANNE-MARIE DARRÉ 1905-1999

Jeanne-Marie Darré: highly regarded for her Saint-Saëns, Chopin and Liszt performances

The renowned French pianist, Jeanne-Marie Darré, died on January 26th at the age of 93. Though her repertoire was large and diverse, she was particularly highly regarded for her Chopin, Saint-Saëns and Liszt. Harold Schonberg once described her thus: 'In her great days she played with a kind of thew and abandon not normally associated with French pianists – and yet she remained quintessentially French: musically sophisticated, rhythmically alert, intelligent, technically flexible and musically charming.'

She was born in Givet in France in 1905 and started playing the piano at the age of five. Initially she was taught by her mother, becoming a student of Marguerite Long at the age of nine when she entered the Paris Conservatoire. It was, however, Isidor Philipp, with whom she studied from the age of 11, who had the most profound influence on her style. 'It was really he who put a stamp on my technique,' she later told an interviewer. If the most frequently recounted event of her life was her performance of all five Saint-Saëns concertos on May 28th, 1926, with the Lamoureux Orchestra under Paul Paray, it was by no means the only example of such stamina. She would think nothing of programming the complete Chopin *Preludes* followed by the *Etudes*, Opp. 10 and 25 for good measure! She recalled once playing a Saint-Saëns concerto for the composer while still working with Philipp (himself a former student of Saint-Saëns). 'He was very boorish, you know, not amiable. He said of me, with his cross air, "this little one, if she works, she will go far. If she doesn't work, if she stops now, all is lost."' Saint-Saëns was not the only significant composer she encountered – she also met and played for Ravel, Fauré and Busoni.

However, it was the 1926 Saint-Saëns concert which launched her international career and the concertos continued to feature prominently in her repertoire for many decades. The recent (and long overdue) reissue of her 1950s HMV recordings was warmly welcomed by Charles Timbrell in these pages (EMI ① CZS5 69470-2, A/97).

Darré initially forged an international career mainly in Europe, only making her American début in 1962, and she continued to play in public until the early 1980s. As well as an extraordinarily busy concert schedule – she liked to play almost every night – she also became a much sought-after teacher at the Paris Conservatoire.

Her playing was characterized by impeccable finger technique, a complete evenness in passagework and a strong sense of rhythm. She attributed her strength to rigorous daily practice of every kind of *étude* and exercise imaginable, a regime she maintained throughout her life.

In addition to the Saint-Saëns concertos, currently available recordings include, on Vanguard Classics, the Liszt B minor Sonata plus shorter works, the complete Chopin *Waltzes*, F minor *Fantasie* and *Berceuse* (reviewed on page 73), the *Preludes* (① OVC8092) and *Scherzos* (① SVC95HD), d'Indy's *Symphonie sur un chant montagnard français* (on Timpani ① 4C4024) and a disc of recordings made in Paris between 1922 and 1947 on VAI (① VAIA1065-2). It is through this small but precious legacy that future generations of piano-lovers will be able to appreciate the art of Jeanne-Marie Darré. **IPQ**

The incomparable Josef Hofmann

ONE OF THE UNDISPUTED GREATS AMONG PIANISTS, JOSEF HOFMANN

(1876-1957) HATED THE COMMERCIAL RECORDING PROCESS. AS A

RESULT, HIS RECORDED LEGACY DERIVES LARGELY FROM LIVE RECITALS

AND RADIO BROADCASTS. **GREGOR BENKO** EXAMINES THE REASONS BEHIND

HOFMANN'S VIEWS AND TRACES HIS CAREER IN AND OUT OF THE STUDIO

Josef Hofmann was 79 in October 1955 when Columbia Records (New York) issued an LP containing portions of his famous 1937 Golden Jubilee Concert. The only commercial records the reclusive pianist had ever allowed to be issued had been made for the American Columbia and Brunswick companies in the outmoded acoustic process, some 30-40 years earlier. Aware that there was scant audible documentation of his art and regretting it deeply, he went to considerable trouble to help Columbia release that first LP of his performances. It included a thick booklet with notes by Hofmann's pupil, Abram Chasins, and the sleeve was wrapped with a gold paper band emblazoned 'Only Available "LP" Recording', together with a quote from Harold Schonberg: 'I would unhesitatingly say that Josef Hofmann was the greatest pianist I ever heard ... Nobody so made the piano sing ... a giant, and his like does not walk the earth today.' Although the packaging was lavish, the LP did not contain the whole concert and was sonically substandard even for the time, but it was nevertheless greeted by the press and public with praise and fanfare.

A few months later Hofmann was dead, and *The New York Times* printed an article with the headline, 'History's Loss – Little of Hofmann's Art Was Recorded Because He Had No Interest in Discs'. Critic Howard Taubman emphasized

the point: 'His passing leaves us with a profound sense of loss which is deepened by the sad knowledge that we have little more than our recollections to remind us of his greatness ... if you wish to rediscover the magic of Hofmann's playing, you can do so on LP only from a single Columbia disc.' Taubman blamed Hofmann 'for this failure' because the pianist refused to make many records. Forty-two years later that situation has been redressed. There are currently six CD volumes available of Hofmann's performances (on VAI and Marston), totalling nine-and-a-half hours of Hofmann recordings, with two more volumes to come which will raise the sum to 13-and-a-half hours. In fact his discography is considerably larger than most of the great pianists whose careers predated the invention of the LP. Quite unique among the pianists of his era, Hofmann's posthumous reputation will probably rest mostly on 'live' recordings stemming from his radio broadcasts and actual recitals.

Live versus studio recordings

Just why Hofmann hated making commercial recordings is unclear. There are some hints about his position to be found in his letters, and we know he felt that an artist had to play differently for the gramophone than for an audience. In an unpublished but revealing essay concerning mechanical pianos, written in 1920, Hofmann stated: 'One must bear in mind that during a pianist's performance two simultaneous impressions are created, tonal and spectacular, and that in a mechanical [recorded] performance only the tonal is produced.' It was this 'spectacular' aspect of music which Hofmann felt an artist owed the audience in live recitals, but which could not be transmitted through mechanical reproduction. This difference is one we can hear when comparing his 1935 unissued HMV records to almost any of his live recordings – the commercial ones are reserved and chaste, much more testaments of thoughtful feeling than his live recordings, which come across as performances rather than thoughts, and celebrate spontaneity and informed emotional insight.

Apart from any concerns Hofmann may have had that his spontaneous style of playing was unsuitable for mechanical reproduction, he was also aware that the trend in musical thought,

A portrait of Josef Hofmann autographed by Thomas Edison

heading by the 1920s towards literalness and the ultra-conservative view of the performer's relationship to the composer and the score, was in contrast to his own playing style. In view of this, it is ironic that Hofmann himself made the very first musical recording – at least by a celebrity artist – in history. The 11-year-old Josef Hofmann was in New York for his sensational prodigy tour in late 1887, just at the time when Edison was at work perfecting a commercial version of his cylinder recording device. On November 25th, 1887, the day that Hofmann arrived in New York, the *New York Evening Post* carried an article entitled 'The Phonograph at Work', which reported 'Within the last week Mr Edison has so far finished some specimens of the type of phonograph which he intends to put on the market next January ... Yesterday Mr. Edison showed the only working phonograph now in his possession to a reporter.' Curiously, young Hofmann's trip to the Edison laboratory was never reported in the press, the visit kept confidential for reasons now unknown. No interviewer ever asked the pianist about this momentous occasion, but reference books were carrying the story during his lifetime and Hofmann never, to my knowledge, repudiated it.

Some misinformed writers (including myself) have suggested that little Jozio (the Polish diminutive for 'Josef') sat on Edison's lap as he recorded the first piano cylinders, but this cannot be true, for we have an 1890 letter from the pianist to Edison pleading with him to speak a few words into a cylinder and send it with a signed photo, 'that I may be able to see you and thanks [to] your great invention hear you too, till I shall be happy enough to make your personal acquaintance.' Clearly Hofmann and Edison had not yet met. The records Hofmann made were probably taken down under the supervision of Edison's private secretary, A. O. Tate, who recalled in his memoirs that 'the development of the phonograph brought to the laboratory in those days many celebrities. Josef Hofmann, a boy prodigy ... was one of these, and he made a number of the earliest records of piano music. In fact, his were the first that were made by any recognized artist ... Josef always prefaced his records with announcement, also recorded, which phonetically sounded like this: "Im-prova-sa-se-on by Yo-sef Of-mann."' Tate added: 'I do not know if they are still in existence. The recording wax cylinders used then were perishable unless extraordinary means were employed to protect them.' Edison's various laboratories, workshops, offices and other facilities are now administered

'Jozio' Hofmann, aged 12. The previous year, 1887, saw him make one of the very earliest recordings

liberty of addressing a few words to you … 4 records with my compositions I presented to the Urania [a scientific supply house/museum in Berlin] and 6 I sent to America.' The letter carries no clue as to the identity of the recipient(s) of the other four cylinders sent to America.

On August 27th Tate wrote to Hofmann again, sending a manual on how to maintain the cylinder recorder together with tips on how to obtain the best results; the letter included two diagrams of how the recording horn should be positioned in relation to the piano. More letters passed back and forth – the original two cylinders of his compositions sent by Hofmann as a gift to Edison never arrived, so in November he sent two more, this time two four-hand compositions of Moszkowski played with his father, Casimir Hofmann. If any early Hofmann cylinders ever do turn up, it is most likely they will be specimens from this group he recorded in Berlin in 1890 and sent to Edison, rather than the very first records from his prodigy tour in late 1887.

by a branch of the federal government and await thorough cataloguing, but there is little chance that these recordings will be found.

Early experiments

Tate corresponded with Hofmann two years later on Edison's behalf, and these letters (many rubber stamped 'taken by phonograph dictation') still exist. In December 1889 Tate wrote to the Edison Phonograph Works that Mr Edison wanted water-motor driven phonographs prepared to be sent as gifts to the Czar of Russia and Josef Hofmann. Although only 14 years old at the time, Hofmann was already an accomplished inventor and had built an automobile and a system of electrical illumination for his home. By March 22nd, 1890 Hofmann had received the machine and wrote the letter thanking Edison and asking for a signed photo cited above. On April 9th Tate responded for Edison: 'He would be very pleased to receive a musical record made by yourself.' Hofmann replied on July 7th: 'I sent two records: a *Szerzo* [sic] and a *Valse*, of my compositions. In the later [sic] one I took the

Hofmann comes of age

Hofmann began playing in public as a mature artist in 1894, at the age of 18. He struggled to establish a career in Europe but was received with little enthusiasm, especially in Germany. However, that singular lack of success was soon overshadowed by the accolades afforded him in Russia, where he soon became the pre-eminent pianist, spoken of everywhere as Rubinstein's successor, even his superior. In Russia, Hofmann and his family were elevated from their humble origins to aristocratic status, and for the next three years Josef spent most of his time there. His celebrity lasted until his final concert in Russia in early 1913, and it is conceivable that he consented at some point to make recordings, perhaps for an obscure label such as Beka or Favorit, and that a presently unknown Hofmann Russian recording might yet turn up.

The first Hofmann performances we can actually hear are five sides he recorded, probably in Berlin, in 1903 when he was 27, for the German branch of the Gramophone & Typewriter Company. These are among the rarest of all piano recordings, and they have

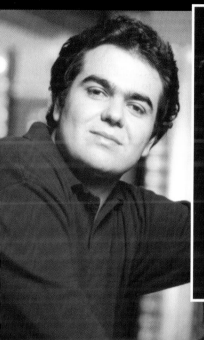
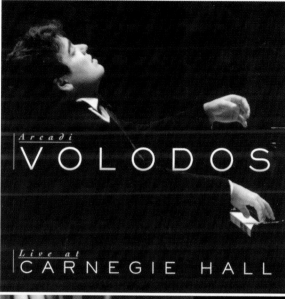

been devotedly transferred to CD (along with other Hofmann recordings discussed here) by master engineer Ward Marston. A decade later Hofmann recorded the same compositions for American Columbia in sound that was little better. In general, the G&Ts are remarkably well-recorded for their time, with the instrument up-front so that one can hear actual piano tone and some nuance. On them, Hofmann's performances are, for the most part, reserved and emotionally neutral, although there are notable rhythmic effects in Tausig's transcription of the Schubert *Marche militaire*.

Hofmann recorded reproducing piano rolls for the German firm of Hupfeld in September 1903, for Welte-Mignon in October 1905 and for Phonola/Triophonola in 1907. He hated these so-called 'recordings', despite his

In Russia, Hofmann was quickly hailed as the new Rubinstein: above, with Alexander Scriabin in Moscow, c1895

apparent endorsement of the Welte rolls: 'What a loss for us that the Mignon was not invented earlier, but what a glorious legacy for the coming generations!' His real opinion was not nearly so sanguine. One longs to hear recordings of Hofmann and the other great pianists at the turn of the century who made rolls of major works – in Hofmann's case there are reproducing roll recordings from this time of Beethoven's Op. 31 No. 3 and Op. 101

Sonatas and the Wagner/Liszt *Tannhäuser* Overture, as well as the usual encore and smaller pieces. But despite the claims of piano-roll enthusiasts, the reproducing mechanism for the Welte and other early companies was too crude to play back many nuances of tone, balance, dynamics or rhythm – and even more damning, the process had no way to record accurately the pianist's individual dynamics and other nuances in the first place. The pianist played, but recorded only his or her keystrokes on the paper roll, along with an editor's approximation of the dynamics, which were inserted simultaneously. Later, the artist could work with the editors to refine the roll but few did. The finished product bore some resemblance to the original performance, but not enough to be described as a 'recording' in the accepted sense of the word – each is more of a reminiscence than a recording. We know that many of the pianists who recorded such rolls and signed extravagant testimonials for them also hated them – Teresa Carreño refused to allow her Welte rolls to be issued when she heard the edited versions played back for the first time, eventually agreeing to their release only when Welte presented her with a luxury car.

The Columbia years

In 1912 Hofmann began an association with American Columbia which lasted for six years. Thirty-three different selections captured by the Columbia acoustic process have come down to us. Six of these were not originally issued, but have survived in the form of test pressings or metal shells in Hofmann's own collection or at Columbia. The issued recordings were originally released on Columbia's very gritty and noisy TriColor banner label discs, and sound very poor when played back on wind-up gramophones. Several of the Columbia recordings were reissued in the late 1920s on superior, quiet pressings which are rare today, and some were available in the form of metal masters to be pressed on vinyl, providing superior sources for audio restoration. Such superior sources are crucial to restoration, as most producers of historic reissues have learned only recently. It took more than 20 years to find these quiet source discs for the Hofmann Columbias. Only then could the resulting CDs be issued properly.

Today we hear detail and tone on these recordings, and there are revelatory things to be found, both musically and pianistically, among Hofmann's Columbias, but one must be able to listen to acoustic recordings with a sense of comfort and ease to appreciate them. Once over that hurdle, listeners can hear (within the limitations of the acoustic process) the awesome power summoned by Hofmann in the Liszt *Tarantella*, an almost unbelievable, immaculate technique in the left hand (without pedal) in the Chopin *Fantaisie-impromptu*, his extraordinarily imaginative and musical way with Chopin *Waltzes*, his other-worldly tonal effects in his own *Sanctuary*, his unparalleled finger technique in Sternberg's C minor *Etude* and his supreme formal and rhythmic genius in the first movement of Beethoven's *Moonlight* Sonata, to list only a few instances.

Hofmann with fellow piano-roll artist Josef Lhévinne in 1936, standing on the deck of the *Majestic* – a boat which Hofmann had designed himself

'Fake' piano rolls

Hofmann's last session for Columbia was on April 7th, 1918, after which he began to record exclusively for the Aeolian Company's Duo Art reproducing piano. He succeeded in negotiating a contract with that firm which guaranteed him $100,000 over a period of years, which he hoped would give his family financial security. How could he have agreed to devote so much effort to the making of inferior roll recordings? $100,000 was an almost unimaginable sum then and the acoustic Columbia recordings sounded dreadfully dim in those days. In addition, the reproducing piano roll process had been greatly improved since Hofmann had recorded his German rolls. There still was no automatic recorder to take down accurately the artist's dynamics and nuances, but he tried to overcome this problem by working extensively with the Duo Art editors to make the finished rolls as good as possible. And he began to experiment himself, eventually inventing a perfected automatic roll recording device in 1929. It was never used, for the Depression killed the piano roll business.

There is much controversy regarding how good or accurate Duo Art rolls are, and whether or not they (unlike the earlier German rolls) can be considered actual 'recordings'. In a letter to Harold Schonberg dated November 11th, 1955

Hofmann had this to say on the subject: 'As regards the Duo-Art rolls … they did well for a while, for at that period the phonograph records were unable to reproduce the piano tone faithfully. Rhythmically they were all correct; dynamically they were a fake. Just the same a certain type of music sounds well, when transferred from the Duo-Art rolls to phono-discs, such as Beethoven's *Turkish March* (transcribed for piano by Anton Rubinstein), Chopin's A flat *Polonaise* – with the exception of the lyric interlude – and even Beethoven's *Rondo a capriccio* in G major, also parts of the *Tannhäuser* Overture: Wagner/ Liszt.'

Musical riches on Brunswick

Hofmann was very proud that he personally (and cannily) negotiated the contract with Aeolian Duo Art, insisting on a clause which allowed him to make phonograph records for other companies, and soon he chose to work with American Brunswick. The original contract has apparently not survived, but from cheque stubs and copies of correspondence we can ascertain that it was a three-year deal beginning in 1923, with Hofmann guaranteeing to record 30 issuable sides or selections and Brunswick paying him $2,000 per side outright, with no royalties. The contract was never completely fulfilled and he made only 16 issued

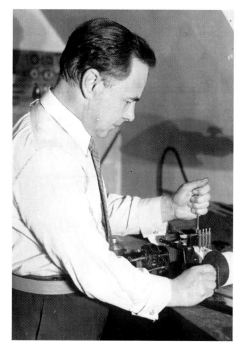

Hofmann spent a great deal of time trying to perfect the art of piano-roll recording by inventing a device for recording musical dynamics: seen at work in his Pennsylvania workshop in 1927

refused to make any more Brunswick records, even to fulfil his contract. The company urged him to re-record some of the same selections in their new beam-of-light electrical process, but it didn't interest him. In truth, this early Brunswick electrical process was very substandard, and records made with it sound worse than Brunswick's late acoustic recordings which antedate them. Perhaps Hofmann might have agreed to make the remaining 14 sides had Brunswick's electrical process been better.

Experimental recordings on RCA

Hofmann's interest in recordings waned at that time as two new interests consumed him – the founding of the Curtis Institute of Music, and a passionate love affair with a young woman who was to become his second wife. There had been no new recordings from him for 12 years when, in about 1935, he recorded his own *Berceuse* on acetate discs for the Curtis Institute to use as a theme tune on its own radio programme. This was done in two versions, one solo and one with a violin obbligato played by Hofmann's colleague at Curtis, Efrem Zimbalist. 1935 also saw two series of recordings made for commercial firms, neither of which were issued at the time. The group recorded for RCA Victor was made in April and May, the London HMV group on November 29th. It must have been around this time that Hofmann became seriously concerned that there wasn't much of a viable legacy in sound and set about doing something about it. The RCA recordings were purely experimental and the particulars have been lost. We know from the memoirs of the company's head of A&R, Charles O'Connell, that the sessions utilized 'electronics and electrical amplification'. O'Connell described these attempts as 'tentative and philosophically erroneous'. No matter what the details of the electronic experiments, today we can hear that the recordings were extremely successful, sounding much better and being more true to real piano tone than RCA's commercial recordings of that time. Later, RCA tried to persuade Hofmann to sign a contract, committing him to make further RCA recordings that could be issued as part of the deal, including the unissued November 1935 HMV recordings. Hofmann never agreed.

sides – but what sides! The Wagner/Brassin *Magic Fire Music* is the most perfect example of orchestral piano playing ever recorded. It was Olga Samaroff who pointed out in a review that part of Hofmann's secret was his realization that the orchestra does not have a pedal. And the Rubinstein *Melody* in F – that threadbare and despised old ball of popcorn – is resurrected through Hofmann's perfect sincerity and simplicity. As the late, beloved piano historian Harry L. Anderson wrote, 'Every time I bring it out again, I listen to it with the same fascinated wonder at the subtle, aristocratic art with which Hofmann converts every note of the thrice-familiar piece into pure gold.'

On the Brunswick discs the acoustic recording method had reached a pinnacle which allowed Hofmann's immortal performances to be captured in an acoustic many feel is more true to the sound of the piano than a lot of recent recordings. Indeed, they are one of the most astonishing achievements in the history of the phonograph. Unfortunately, Hofmann

In retrospect O'Connell seems to have been remarkably uncomprehending and conceited. He is the man who turned down Rachmaninov's request that RCA record several of his live recitals. He is the man who wrote in his 1947 autobiography: 'The piano builder and the piano composer have then both played into the hands of the mere virtuoso, who in turn plays to the most primitive instincts of the public ... the piano ... a vehicle for the exploitation of the (to me) insufferable brilliance of Horowitz, the desiccated didacticism of Schnabel, the preciosity of Hofmann, the archness of Iturbi.' Hofmann wouldn't have liked this man very much, and never signed a contract with RCA for these experimental sides either, legally assuring that RCA wouldn't own the rights or be able to issue them. The group contains some rather uncommitted performances and even some wrong notes, but it also contains a complete first movement of the Chopin Third Sonata in a calm and unhurried performance of lapidary tonal beauty ('transcendent lyricism' wrote Harold Schonberg) and perfect formal understanding.

The perfect Hofmann records

Unlike the RCA group, the HMV recordings were not experiments but recorded by the company in the hope that Hofmann would agree to their release. We know from his later correspondence that he thought these to be the most perfect records he had ever made and wanted them to be issued at some point. But for some mysterious reason he wouldn't sign a contract with HMV and the discs remained unissued for decades. In the early 1960s the producers of the 'Great Recordings of the Century' LPs wanted to include them in that series on a disc that was to contain the extant Busoni recordings as well – an excellent idea. EMI had vinyl pressings made from the shells. These pressings were then tape-recorded with filtering, and, as was the custom at that time, the original masters and the vinyl pressings were destroyed! Eventually the idea to issue the recordings was abandoned – EMI did not have a contract with Hofmann.

One has to agree with Hofmann himself that these are the best of his records, each

'Drag artists': Josef Hofmann with Leopold Stokowski in fancy dress at the birthday party of friend Mary Bok in 1916

performance a masterpiece in his 'gramophone' (non-spectacular) style. Most connoisseurs prefer the two Chopin/Liszt transcriptions, but for me it is the Beethoven sonata movement which takes pride of place. What a wealth of information it contains about the way Beethoven was played before our modern, anti-historical conventions of performance practice took hold.

From 1935 onwards, Hofmann and his managers regularly received inquiries from record companies begging the pianist to consider recording whatever he wanted for their label. He did visit a few record company studios to test results of their individual recording processes, always making one disc only, always the same 'test pattern' disc, a sequence of the opening bars of a Chopin *polonaise*, *waltz* and *nocturne* plus the complete, short *Musical snuffbox* of Liadov. He felt this sequence tested every aspect of piano recording, and found each company's process wanting, at least to the extent that he wasn't tempted to make further recordings. There is no clear evidence as to why this was the case – probably he felt a tension, wanting to leave a recorded legacy but knowing his style was already historical. And he was experiencing a lot of turmoil in his personal life which must have taken precedence over philosophical questions about recording.

Concert and radio recordings

In 1937 Hofmann's managers and friends convinced him to undertake a Golden Jubilee Tour, commemorating the 50th anniversary of his professional début in America. The highlight of the tour was the concert on November 28th, 1937, in New York's Metropolitan Opera House, where he had first appeared on November 29th, 1887. That concert, which featured the Curtis Student Orchestra under Fritz Reiner, was one of the most famous of our century and was recorded in its entirety. Hofmann's wife hired RCA Custom Recordings (a division of the record label) to make the recordings at a cost of $1,837·45, covering standby electricians at the Metropolitan, transportation, ATT wires, 11 16-inch 33⅓ masters, 26 12-inch 78rpm masters and 156 pressed records – six sets of the 12-inch pressed records. RCA cheated a bit, and made original recordings on the 16-inch 33⅓ discs only, dubbing the 12-inch 78rpm discs from the larger ones. These dubs were pressed on shellac with special white and gold labels and were used by the Hofmanns as gifts for friends. Hofmann donated the proceeds of

On stage at the Met: above, reading congratulatory telegrams immediately after his Golden Jubilee Concert, November 28th, 1937

the concert, over $20,000, to the Musician's Emergency Relief Fund.

Just four months later the pianist gave his farewell recital at his beloved Curtis Institute of Music in Casimir Hall, named after his father. That concert – a very emotional occasion – was recorded almost by accident. This recording of his 'spectacular' (in Hofmann's sense) performances of Beethoven's *Waldstein* Sonata and Chopin's E flat minor *Polonaise* and F minor *Ballade* is among the legendary piano recordings, fervently loved by many and heartily despised by others.

The next ten years of Hofmann's career, his last performing decade, produced no commercial recordings. He did play frequently on the radio, and it is from acetate discs made from these broadcasts that a significant portion of his discography stems. From these non-commercial and broadcast recordings we can single out the performances of the Rubinstein D minor Concerto from the Golden Jubilee Concert, the two Chopin concertos, the Beethoven Fourth Concerto with John Barbirolli (not yet Sir John), the Chopin C minor *Nocturne* from a 1945 Carnegie Hall recital, a complete Beethoven *Moonlight* Sonata from a 1936 broadcast, and of course the Casimir Hall performances mentioned earlier, as cornerstones of recorded art and object lessons in romantic pianism.

The final years

After his retirement Hofmann had an unhappy life, the last years of which were spent largely in solitude and silence. He worked ceaselessly, trying to perfect a better method of recording the piano, in connection with which he had a home acetate cutter and a Steinway baby grand. He experimented with different pieces of equipment and with all kinds of novel ideas, bolting speakers and then microphones to various parts of the piano. With only one exception, these experimental home recordings were always of the aforementioned 'piano recording test pattern', ending with the Liadov *Musical snuffbox*. That one exception is a gem, the complete Gluck/Sgambati 'Mélodie' from *Orfeo*, probably recorded in 1948.

As he approached the age of 80, Hofmann began to pursue with urgency the idea of sponsoring some recording of his art. When Columbia Records contacted him in early 1955, inquiring about the possibility of their issuing some of the recordings of the Golden Jubilee Concert, he willingly co-operated. A huge problem presented itself, however, when RCA Victor refused to turn over the masters of the recordings, claiming that the ownership of them was in doubt and that it probably owned the rights. Hofmann knew he had paid for the records and that RCA was wrong, but could not produce the documentation (it was, and still is, extant, but was at that time in the home of his estranged wife). Eventually Columbia made its mastertapes from Hofmann's set of the 78rpm 12-inch discs which, as we have seen, were dubs of the 16-inch originals. Hofmann specifically excluded his performances of the Chopin A flat *Waltz* and F sharp major *Nocturne* from the material he authorized Columbia to issue, explaining that these were selections he had recorded in 1935 for HMV and he didn't want to permit anything which might jeopardize the possibility of his favourite records eventually being commercially issued. Columbia also omitted all the concerted numbers and Walter Damrosch's speech.

During these last months Hofmann was also contacted by a colourful New York record producer, Edward J. Smith, who had started a company named the Record Corporation of America (which, not necessarily incidentally or innocently, allowed Smith to abbreviate his company name to 'RCA'). Smith wanted to issue some of Hofmann's Duo Art rolls on LP. The pianist agreed to work on experiments with Smith. Tapes of some of the rolls were made on a Duo Art piano and sent to Hofmann, along with very enlarged copies of the scores of the works represented – Hofmann's sight was deteriorating. He listened to the roll recordings and simultaneously added dynamic markings to the enlarged scores, indicating expression to be added to the recordings. Smith proposed to accomplish this by simply raising and lowering the volume level of the amplifier playing back the tapes at the indicated spots in a fashion that would approximate to Hofmann's markings. Smith enlisted the aid of the piano historian and Hofmann fanatic Jan Holcman to do the actual dial turning.

Hofmann was often over-medicated and even intoxicated at the end of his life, and his condition could be one answer to the question of how he could have participated in this dubious scheme with Smith. A letter sent to Smith a few weeks before he died indicates that he actually liked the results. Another answer to that question could possibly be that he knew time was short and was grasping at straws in an attempt to leave some kind of recorded artistic heritage. The project was incomplete at the time of his death. Holcman and Smith fought for two years, especially when Smith decided he wanted to issue tapes he had obtained of all of Hofmann's late Bell Telephone broadcasts, many of which Holcman felt to be substandard. Eventually an LP of the Duo Art transfers with the boosted dynamics was issued on one of Smith's labels in the early 1960s, and another Smith LP presented some Bell Telephone and Ford Hour Hofmann broadcast recordings. The Duo Art transfers sound dreadful.

Hofmann's actual playing, as revealed on record, is the subject of much controversy today. Some of the wisest positive commentary can be found in a 1985 review by Will Crutchfield: 'His personal style, rooted in 19th-century assumptions about music, was on its way out of favor, and after the final, troubled phase of his public activity, his name and way of playing were set to one side by the shapers of postwar musical opinion. He himself was not forgotten, but what he embodied was ... his ways and means were those of the Romantic late 19th century, and that ultimately cost him his standing – but his survival so long against the tide is attributable in part to a spirit that had little in common with popular perceptions of Romantic sentimentality. His playing was both virile and delicate, finely detailed yet swept along on an intense, surging current; there was a force of musical rhetoric that apparently could be overwhelming in concert, and can still be, on records. It should not be missed.'IPQ

All photographs courtesy of Gregor Benko

Gregor Benko was co-founder of the International Piano Archives and has been co-producer of each volume of the compact disc series, 'The Complete Josef Hofmann'. He is currently working on a biography of the pianist.

Review of 'The Complete Josef Hofmann', Volume 6 on page 99

The Complete
Josef Hofmann
Vol.6

THE CASIMIR HALL RECITAL

Also included on this, the sixth in a series of eight volumes of the complete works of Josef Hofmann is a previously unissued Beethoven "Moonlight" Sonata (1936 Broadcast) and the 1941 Beethoven 4th Piano Concerto (1941 Broadcast).

52014-2

the
Complete
Record Company
Ltd
0171-498 9666

www.marstonrecords.com

JOSEF HOFMANN: THE COMPLETE DISCOGRAPHY

Compiled by Farhan Malik

Work	Matrix	Issue	Source or Venue (Conductor)	Date
Beethoven				
Concerto No. 4, Op. 58		IPL ☉ 503	Philadelphia (Ormandy)	4/4/38*
		Marston ① 52014	New York (Barbirolli)	26/10/41*
		Unpublished	New York (Mitropoulos)	22/8/43*
Concerto No. 5, Op. 73		Eklipse ① 1405	Chicago (Lange)	12/5/40*
		CSO ① 90-3		
1st mvt**		Unpublished	Bell Telephone Hour (Voorhees)	19/8/46*
3rd mvt		IPA ☉ 502	Ford Hour (Iturbi)	10/19/41*
3rd mvt**		Allegro ☉ 1711	Bell Telephone Hour (Voorhees)	9/8/43*
Sonata, Op. 27 No. 2 [cpte]		Marston ① 52014	Cadillac Hour	15/3/36*
1st mvt	48946-4	VAI ① 1036	Columbia Unpublished	13/10/16
		Marston ① 52014		
1st mvt	48946-5	Marston ① 52014	Columbia Unpublished	13/10/16
1st mvt		Marston ① 52014	Bell Telephone Hour	31/7/44*
Sonata, Op. 31 No. 3 –				
2nd mvt	2EA 2579-1	Marston ① 52004	HMV Unpublished	29/11/35
Sonata, Op. 53		Marston ① 52014	Casimir Hall	7/4/38*
Beethoven/Rubinstein				
Turkish March	10505	VAI ① 1047	Brunswick	1923
		VAI ① 1020	Met Op Golden Jubilee	28/11/37*
Chopin				
Andante spianato and				
Grand Polonaise, Op. 22		VAI ① 1020	Met Op Golden Jubilee	28/11/37*
		Marston ① 52004	Philadelphia Golden Jubilee	4/4/38*
		VAI ① 1020	Carnegie Hall	24/3/45*
Ballade, Op. 23		VAI ① 1020	Met Op Golden Jubilee	28/11/37*
Ballade, Op. 52		Marston ① 52014	Casimir Hall	7/4/38*
Berceuse, Op. 57	49327-3	VAI ① 1036	Columbia	26/3/18
		VAI ① 1020	Met Op Golden Jubilee	28/11/37*
		Marston ① 52004	Philadelphia Golden Jubilee	4/4/38*
		Unpublished	Bell Telephone Hour	13/1/47*
Concerto No. 1, Op. 11		VAI ① 1002	New York (Barbirolli)	13/3/38*
1st mvt**		VAI ① 1002	BBC (Harty)	6/11/35*
3rd mvt		Eklipse ① 1405	Bell Telephone Hour (Voorhees)	31/7/44*
Concerto No. 2, Op. 21		VAI ① 1002	New York (Barbirolli)	27/12/36*
2nd mvt		Eklipse ① 1405	Bell Telephone Hour (Voorhees)	30/7/45*
Etude, Op. 25 No. 9		VAI ① 1020	Met Op Golden Jubilee	28/11/37*
		Unpublished	Bell Telephone Hour	31/7/44*
Fantaisie-impromptu, Op. 66	49326-2	VAI ① 1036	Columbia	6/3/18
Impromptu, Op. 29	48979-3	VAI ① 1036	Columbia Unpublished	3/11/16
	48979-1	Unpublished	Columbia Unpublished	3/11/16
Mazurka, Op. 33 No. 3		VAI ① 1020	Carnegie Hall	24/3/45*
Nocturne, Op. 9 No. 2	30749-?	VAI ① 1036	Columbia	4/4/12
		VAI ① 1020	Met Op Golden Jubilee	28/11/37*
		Marston ① 52004	Ford Hour	19/10/41*
Nocturne, Op. 9 No. 3		Marston ① 52014	Casimir Hall	7/4/38*
Nocturne, Op. 15 No. 2	X10420	VAI ① 1047	Brunswick	1923
	2EA 2578-1	Marston ① 52004	HMV Unpublished	29/11/35
		Marston ① 52014	Cadillac Hour	15/3/36*

Title	Matrix	Label	Source	Date
		VAI Ⓟ 1020	Met Op Golden Jubilee	28/11/37*
		Marston Ⓟ 52004	Philadelphia Golden Jubilee	4/4/38*
		Marston Ⓟ 52004	Bell Telephone Hour	9/8/43*
Nocturne, Op. 27 No. 2	CS 88938-1**	Marston Ⓟ 52004	RCA Victor Unpublished	2/5/35
	CS 88938-2	Marston Ⓟ 52004	RCA Victor Unpublished	6/5/35
		Marston Ⓟ 52004	Damrosch Birthday Broadcast	1/1/42*
	CO 26504-1**	Marston Ⓟ 52004	Columbia Test	9/2/40
Nocturne, Op. 48 No. 1		VAI Ⓟ 1020	Carnegie Hall	24/3/45*
Polonaise, Op. 26 No. 2		Marston Ⓟ 52014	Casimir Hall	7/4/38*
Polonaise, Op. 40 No. 1	1711X	VAI Ⓟ 1036	G&T	1903
	36359-1	VAI Ⓟ 1036	Columbia	8/4/12
	10336	VAI Ⓟ 1047	Brunswick	1923
	CS 88961-1	Marston Ⓟ 52004	RCA Victor Unpublished	6/5/35
		Unpublished	Bell Telephone Hour	1/3/43*
	CO 26504-1**	Marston Ⓟ 52004	Columbia Test	9/2/40
Scherzo, Op. 20**	X10455	VAI Ⓟ 1047	Brunswick	1923
Sonata, Op. 58 – 1st mvt	CS 88959/60-1	Marston Ⓟ 52004	RCA Victor Unpublished	6/5/35
Waltz, Op. 18		Marston Ⓟ 52014	Casimir Hall	7/4/38*
		Marston Ⓟ 52004	Bell Telephone Hour	9/8/43*
Waltz, Op. 34 No. 1	49306-1	VAI Ⓟ 1036	Columbia	13/2/18
		VAI Ⓟ 1020	Carnegie Hall	24/3/45*
Waltz, Op. 42	CS 88937-1	Marston Ⓟ 52004	RCA Victor Unpublished	19/4/35
	CS 88962-1	Marston Ⓟ 52004	RCA Victor Unpublished	19/4/35
	CS 88937-2	Marston Ⓟ 52004	RCA Victor Unpublished	2/5/35
	CS 88937-4	Marston Ⓟ 52004	RCA Victor Unpublished	2/5/35
	2EA 2575-1	Marston Ⓟ 52004	HMV Unpublished	29/11/35
		Marston Ⓟ 52014	Cadillac Hour	15/3/36*
		VAI Ⓟ 1020	Met Op Golden Jubilee	28/11/37*
		Unpublished	Bell Telephone Hour	14/1/46*
	CO 26504-1**	Marston Ⓟ 52004	Columbia Test	9/2/40
Waltz, Op. 64 No. 1		Marston Ⓟ 52014	Cadillac Hour	15/3/36*
		VAI Ⓟ 1020	Met Op Golden Jubilee	28/11/37*
		Marston Ⓟ 52004	Philadelphia Golden Jubilee	4/4/38*
		Marston Ⓟ 52004	Ford Hour	19/10/41*
		Marston Ⓟ 52004	Damrosch Birthday Broadcast	1/1/42*
		Unpublished	Bell Telephone Hour	9/8/43*
(arr. Hofmann)		Marston Ⓟ 52014	Casimir Hall	7/4/38*
Waltz, Op. 64 No. 2	48977-3	VAI Ⓟ 1036	Columbia Unpublished	2/11/16
	48977-1	Unpublished	Columbia Unpublished	2/11/16
	48977-2	Unpublished	Columbia Unpublished	2/11/16
	X10405	VAI Ⓟ 1047	Brunswick	1923
Waltz in E minor, Op. posth	36357-1	VAI Ⓟ 1036	Columbia	8/4/12
	48977-4	VAI Ⓟ 1036	Columbia Unpublished	2/11/16
Chopin/Liszt				
Maiden's Wish	49328-2	VAI Ⓟ 1036	Columbia	6/3/18
	CS 88958-1	Marston Ⓟ 52004	RCA Victor Unpublished	6/5/35
	2EA 2577-1	Marston Ⓟ 52004	HMV Unpublished	29/11/35
My Joys	X10503	VAI Ⓟ 1047	Brunswick	1923
	2EA 2576-1	Marston Ⓟ 52004	HMV Unpublished	29/11/35
Debussy				
Clair de lune		Marston Ⓟ 52004	Bell Telephone Hour	19/8/46*
Dillon				
Birds at Dawn	49619-2	VAI Ⓟ 1036	Columbia	7/4/18

Gluck/Brahms

Gavotte	48951-3	VAI ℗ 1036	Columbia Unpublished	13/10/16
	10107	VAI ℗ 1047	Brunswick	1923

Gluck/Sgambati

Mélodie		Marston ℗ 52004	Home Recording	c1948

Grieg

Papillon, Op. 43 No. 1	48949-1	VAI ℗ 1036	Columbia	13/10/16
	47134-1	VAI ℗ 1036	Columbia	4/11/16

Hofmann

Berceuse, Op. 20 No. 5		Marston ℗ 52004	Curtis Institute	c1935
with violin (Zimbalist)		Marston ℗ 52004	Curtis Institute	c1935
Chromaticon		VAI ℗ 1020	Curtis Institute (Hilsberg)	6/9/37*
		VAI ℗ 1020	Met Op Golden Jubilee (Reiner)	28/11/37*
Elegy		Marston ℗ 52004	Bell Telephone Hour	1/3/43*
Kaleidoskop, Op. 40 No. 4		Marston ℗ 52014	Casimir Hall	7/4/38*
Nocturne	10368	VAI ℗ 1047	Brunswick	1923
Penguine		Marston ℗ 52014	Casimir Hall	7/4/38*
Sanctuary	37465-1	VAI ℗ 1036	Columbia Unpublished	8/11/15

Liadov

Musical Snuffbox, Op. 32	CO 26504-1	Marston ℗ 52004	Columbia Test	9/2/40
		Unpublished	Bell Telephone Hour	9/8/43*
		Unpublished	Bell Telephone Hour	14/1/46*

Liszt

Hungarian Rhapsody No. 2	X9431, X9434	VAI ℗ 1047	Brunswick	12/1922
	X10488**	VAI ℗ 1047	Brunswick	1923
La campanella	0873	VAI ℗ 1047	Brunswick Unpublished	c1917
Liebestraum No. 3	36358-1	VAI ℗ 1036	Columbia	8/4/12
		Marston ℗ 52004	Ford Hour	19/10/41*
Tarantella**	48976-2	VAI ℗ 1036	Columbia	2/11/16
Waldesrauschen	49363-2	VAI ℗ 1036	Columbia	26/3/18
	10105	VAI ℗ 1047	Brunswick	1923

Mendelssohn

Hunting Song, Op. 19 No. 3	1709 1/2	VAI ℗ 1036	G&T	1903
	49307-2	VAI ℗ 1036	Columbia	14/2/18
Rondo capriccioso, Op. 14	49309-3**	VAI ℗ 1036	Columbia	13/2/18
		Marston ℗ 52004	Bell Telephone Hour	27/3/44*
		Unpublished	Bell Telephone Hour	13/1/47*
Spring Song, Op. 62 No. 6	1710 1/2X	VAI ℗ 1036	G&T	1903
	19847-1	VAI ℗ 1036	Columbia	5/4/12
		Unpublished	Bell Telephone Hour	30/7/45*
Spinning Song, Op. 67 No. 4	48949-1	VAI ℗ 1036	Columbia	13/10/16
	47135-1	VAI ℗ 1036	Columbia	4/11/16
		VAI ℗ 1020	Met Op Golden Jubilee	28/11/37*
		Marston ℗ 52004	Philadelphia Golden Jubilee	4/4/38*
		Unpublished	Bell Telephone Hour	19/8/46*

Moszkowski

La Jongleuse, Op. 52 No. 4	49307-2	VAI ℗ 1036	Columbia	14/2/18
Capriccio espagnole, Op. 37	48948-5**	VAI ℗ 1036	Columbia	16/10/16
		VAI ℗ 1020	Met Op Golden Jubilee	28/11/37*

Paderewski

Minuet, Op. 14 No. 1	48975-2	VAI ℗ 1036	Columbia	2/11/16

Parker

Valse Gracile, Op. 49 No. 3	49619-2	VAI ℗ 1036	Columbia	7/4/18

Prokofiev

Marche, Op. 12 No. 1		Marston ① 52004	Bell Telephone Hour	1/3/43*
		Unpublished	Bell Telephone Hour	19/8/46*
Rachmaninov				
Prelude, Op. 3 No. 2	30747-2	VAI ① 1036	Columbia	4/4/12
	49620-2	VAI ① 1036	Columbia	7/4/18
	10433	VAI ① 1047	Brunswick	1923
		Marston ① 52004	Bell Telephone Hour	1/3/43*
Prelude, Op. 23 No. 5	37467-1	VAI ① 1036	Columbia	8/11/15
	X10434	VAI ① 1047	Brunswick	1923
		VAI ① 1020	Met Op Golden Jubilee	28/11/37*
		Unpublished	Bell Telephone Hour	30/7/45*
Rubinstein				
Concerto No. 3		IPA ⊙ 500	New York (Rodzinski)	5/3/44*
Concerto No. 4		VAI ① 1020	Met Op Golden Jubilee (Reiner)	28/11/37*
		Eklipse ① 1405	Detroit (Kruger)	10/3/45*
1st mvt**		Unpublished	Bell Telephone Hour (Voorhees)	27/3/44*
3rd mvt		Unpublished	Bell Telephone Hour (Voorhees)	1/3/43*
El Dachtarawan, Op. 93 No. 9	37465-1	VAI ① 1036	Columbia Unpublished	8/11/15
Melody in F, Op. 3 No. 1	10436	VAI ① 1047	Brunswick	1923
Valse caprice	30999-1	VAI ① 1036	Columbia	6/4/12
Scarlatti/Tausig				
Capriccio, Kk20	X10352	VAI ① 1047	Brunswick	1923
Pastorale, Kk9	X10352	VAI ① 1047	Brunswick	1923
Schubert/Godowsky				
Moment musical No. 3		Marston ① 52014	Casimir Hall	7/4/38*
Schubert/Liszt				
Erlkönig	49	VAI ① 1036	G&T	1903
	48945-4	VAI ① 1036	Columbia	13/10/16
Schubert/Tausig				
Marche militaire	4½**	VAI ① 1036	G&T	1903
	30750-2**	VAI ① 1036	Columbia	4/4/12
Schumann				
Concerto, Op. 54				
1st mvt**		Eklipse ① 1405	Bell Telephone Hour (Voorhees)	13/1/47*
3rd mvt		Eklipse ① 1405	Bell Telephone Hour (Voorhees)	14/1/46*
Kreisleriana, Op. 16**		Marston ① 52014	Casimir Hall	7/4/38*
Warum?, Op. 12 No. 3	19848-1	VAI ① 1036	Columbia	8/4/12
Sternberg				
Etude, Op. 120 No. 3	37445-1	VAI ① 1036	Columbia	8/11/15
Stojowski				
Caprice orientale, Op. 10 No. 2		Marston ① 52014	Casimir Hall	7/4/38*
Wagner/Brassin				
Magic Fire Music	X10502	VAI ① 1047	Brunswick	1923
Weber				
Sonata No. 1 – Perpetuum mobile		Marston ① 52004	Ford Hour	19/10/41*

Notes

Date followed by * denotes live recording

Date followed by ** denotes an excerpt, abridged or incomplete recording

1) An interview from 21/1/52 was released on VAI ① 1002

2) Several more discs exist containing Hofmann's test pattern (fragments from Chopin: Nocturne, Op. 27 No. 2, Polonaise, Op. 40 No. 1, Waltz, Op. 42 and the complete Liadov Musical Snuffbox)

Special thanks to Gregor Benko and Donald Manildi for their assistance in compiling this discography

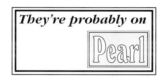

Dancing with the Unknown

Harriet Smith interviews one of the most individual pianists of his generation, Piotr Anderszewski. Though he can boast a busy concert schedule, he has yet to make his name on record

The name Piotr Anderszewski first came to my attention through his spectacular performances – and no-less spectacular self-disqualification – from the semi-finals of the 1990 Leeds International Piano Competition. It is not something any artist would relish being remembered for – walking off-stage in the middle of Webern's aphoristic Op. 27 Variations (lasting little over five minutes), especially after having completed an epic rendition of the *Diabellis*. Such drama was due not to nerves but to a highly developed sense of self-criticism: he wasn't satisfied, so he simply stopped.

Nine years on, Anderszewski remains very much his own man, an artist who is attracting a growing band of enthusiastic *aficionados*. Attending his recitals, which are crafted as painstakingly as the most exquisitely-wrought menu, offers a breath of fresh air, events where one can expect the unexpected. At his most recent Wigmore Hall recital he presented a programme of Beethoven's *Diabelli* Variations, Szymanowski's *Métopes* and Bach's Fifth *French Suite*. He greeted the enthusiastic applause with something more substantial than the usual *petits fours* – Bach's B minor *French Overture*, no less, with all repeats observed. It was a fitting conclusion to a joyous occasion. If some of the audience were nonplussed by the 35-minute encore, they'd have been even more surprised had Anderszewski carried out his original plan. 'I wasn't very happy with the way the *Diabellis* went,' he told me afterwards in the green room, 'so I was contemplating repeating them as an encore.' Was he joking? Not a bit of it – when this pianist is absorbed, he expects no less of his audience, though on this occasion the

Piotr Anderszewski: 'We are being invaded by such a quantity of recordings: who needs more of them?' *Photo Gruszka*

inadequacies of London's public transport system proved the final arbiter.

Despite a busy international concert schedule, a recording contract has so far eluded Anderszewski. His discography numbers a mere three chamber discs – two on Philips with the Russian violinist Viktoria Mullova and one on CD Accord with his sister, Dorota, also a violinist – and until recently only a single solo recital, of Bach, Beethoven and Webern, on Polish PolyGram. Now Harmonia Mundi has included him in its Les Nouveaux Interprètes series, with a disc of Bach. Is this dearth of recordings also a result of his hyper self-criticism?

'Well, we are being invaded by such a quantity of recordings: who needs more of them? I believe that unless one has something really special to say that has not been said before, there is no point releasing the 999th version of a Beethoven sonata. I now feel mature enough to put down the *Diabellis* and would like to do it before I reach 30. I'd also like to record more Bach. And Szymanowski – that's my new discovery and I absolutely adore his music.'

Try asking most musicians about the recording process and they trot out all the old clichés about long takes being preferable to short ones, the fewer edits the better, the challenge of recording being to recreate the atmosphere of a concert. Not so Anderszewski. 'They are two different professions. During a concert, every second is unique, the process is irreversible. Besides the quality of the playing, other uncontrollable parameters come into play. That's the magic of it! In a studio the time is broken up, you know you can repeat things so time ceases to matter – it's a much more cerebral occupation. The idea of less editing being automatically better is complete rubbish. You need to build something objective and something that will endure. Similarly, trying to make a recording that is a vague imitation of a performance is pointless: the recording process is artificial and it's important to accept that and to make something completely different out of it – to treat it almost as a different art form.'

> '*Trying to make a recording that is a vague imitation of a performance is pointless: the recording process is artificial and it's important to accept that and to make something completely different out of it – to treat it almost as a different art form.*'

If Anderszewski found that a piece wasn't going the way he intended on-stage, presumably he wouldn't now walk off. Had his views on what constituted 'acceptable' now broadened?

'Yes. It's something I've come to terms with – that what one feels on-stage and what I want to hear with hours and days and months of practising and searching is one thing and what the public feels is something totally different. Years ago at Leeds, one of my problems was not being able to differentiate between these two things. Slowly one discovers that there is not one absolute truth, there are many. People come to a concert with a particular expectation; I've got to respect this expectation even though it may be completely different from my own. The stage and the audience are two different worlds and the way links are being made between them is unexpected and irrational.'

So presumably the idea that it is possible to arrive at a particular interpretation that is preferable to all others no longer applies? 'A few years ago I was convinced there *was* one truth: in the *Diabellis*, for example. The idea of performing it any other way would have been insupportable, so I had to know exactly how I wanted to play every single note. Now I'm just trying to let things happen, and happen on-stage too, playing with the unknown, if you like. I'm much happier taking this approach because even if you have prepared everything perfectly you can never predict exactly what will happen on-stage, how you will feel, what the piano will be like, the hall, the audience … That's the greatest fun, to dance with this unknown and to discover something new every time; it offers endless possibilities.'

As that early appearance at Leeds might indicate, Anderszewksi doesn't take the obvious route when it comes to programme planning. I recall the BBC presenter at the time being rather nonplussed by his massively lopsided semi-final programme of the *Diabellis* and the Webern Variations. 'There are obviously links: both are cycles of variations, both are incredibly intense, and both pieces are peaks in the piano output of their respective composers (though with Webern, of course, it's practically the only piece). In my opinion, the *Diabellis* are Beethoven's most elaborate, rich, dense and at the same time humorous piano piece.' Not for Anderszewski the tyranny of *intégrales*: 'Just filling in empty spaces because it will look serious on the CD cover or in the programme – I think that's terrible. What an imbalance between form and content!'

Critics have also drawn attention to Anderszewski's penchant for rigorously structured pieces, not just the variation form as witnessed through Beethoven and Webern, but also the contrapuntal and fugal complexities of Bach. Was he comfortable with the 'cerebral' tag? 'Of course I want to understand what I play, but neither pure intellect nor pure instinct would work. It has be to a blend of both – that's what is so difficult to achieve, and on the rare occasions when it happens it's the greatest feeling! Just as you could say that reading a book about the structure of, say, the *Diabellis* might be helpful, so might a dramatic life experience: it's always a game of paradoxes with a very thin line between being open-minded and yet not influenced by everything.'

Talking of influences, Anderszewski reveals an interestingly diverse trio who made a profound impression on him early on. 'Richter influenced me enormously. Before I could even speak I was listening to his records – and Glenn Gould. I was completely taken by his genius. I listen to very few records these days, but at a certain point in your life I think it's very important. Michelangeli is the other pianist I most admire. There are many, many that I adore, but those three stand out.'

And could it be that some of his freedom and *joie de vivre*, particularly in the music of Bach, comes indirectly from Gould? 'With Bach I think you have the most joy and freedom, though within certain rules. With Webern you have to be very strict – his music demands crystal clarity. Respecting the text means something different with every composer: a *forte* in Mozart, in Beethoven, in Rachmaninov are of course completely different things. And what do you mean by this *forte*? In relation to what? The most important thing is that the whole thing has an inner sense and that all the elements work together. Just playing literally what's on the page is no guarantee of success. And of course the more knowledge you have, the more paths you have to choose from. The important thing is not to create difficulties where there aren't any. Interpreting music on the piano is a very hard thing to do, especially now, because there's such a weight of truly great historical artists. For a musician to find his own language is a bit like Brahms writing his First Symphony after those of Beethoven. It takes lots of courage and lots of pain sometimes but you have to go through it. If you start to question everything you end up not being able to do anything at all. Take Szymanowski – there are so many notes! Memory is a real difficulty with him. If you begin to think, "how come I can remember all of this?", you become completely paralysed. So a balance is important. Questioning, yes, but not to the point where one can't function.'

Could this difficulty be the reason for Szymanowski's relative neglect? 'Everyone says that Szymanowski *should* be played much more. And yet he's not, perhaps because his music does demand a lot of time and patience. This music is

'For a musician to find his own language is a bit like Brahms writing his First Symphony after those of Beethoven.'
Photo Noelle

all about atmosphere. The moment you stop playing the notes and let yourself be taken by it, all those dense harmonies, strange dissonances and capricious moods become obvious and clear. It means you're ready. But it takes a lot of time, to stop playing the notes.'

Anderszewski is impatient to record a disc of Szymanowski's music, which would undoubtedly be a major addition to the discography. 'At the moment, I'm in the process of learning the *Masques*, so it's time to be patient!' He is set to combine them with some of the *Mazurkas* at the Brighton Festival this May and then with Bach in America and the Lebanon.

I finished the interview with a standard question, 'Did he have an overriding artistic ambition?', wondering what kind of answer it would provoke. And he didn't disappoint. 'One of my dreams is to conduct Beethoven's *Missa solemnis*. I studied conducting in the States and for years that has been a goal. I'd need lots of rehearsals, so that it was really as I wanted it. So far, there hasn't been a perfect recording of it – maybe that's not possible. The idea is so elevated. It is not only how high he goes but also what it takes him to climb up there – it's almost impossible. But that's one of my most cherished dreams … one day.' IPQ

Review of Anderszewski's Bach recital on page 66

When the playing had to stop

TALENT CAN BE A HARD CROSS TO BEAR. **BRYCE MORRISON** RELATES THE

CAUTIONARY TALE OF THE PRODIGIOUSLY GIFTED EILEEN JOYCE

WHO GAVE OUT SO MUCH IN HER 25 YEARS OF PUBLIC PLAYING THAT SHE

FOUND SHE LOST TRACK OF HER SELF

Celebrated for the wrong reasons, Eileen Joyce is chiefly remembered as a 'popular' pianist who excelled in a war-horse repertoire (with countless performances of, say, the Grieg and Schumann Concertos to her credit) and whose habit of changing her dress to suit composer, mood and occasion (blue for Beethoven, green for Chopin, black and a dangling, outsize crucifix after the death of King George VI and a request that 'you all join with me and say a little prayer while I play *Jesu, joy of man's desiring*') left her a tattered reputation and an undistinguished, sadly misleading entry in the current *Grove*.

The cautionary tale of Eileen Joyce's rise to a glittering if temporary status is both exhilarating and disturbing. Born in a tent in Zeehan, Tasmania, she grew up in Western Australia, of Irish-Spanish descent and the daughter of an itinerant, gold-prospecting labourer. Unaffectionately known as 'Ragged Eilee', she ran barefoot through the Bush accompanied by Twink, her beloved pet kangaroo and, finding herself blessed with rare and improbable musical instincts, desperately sought an outlet for her talent. A few notes heard on a friend's mouth-organ, the sight of a frustratingly inaccessible piano in a shop window, and her future was sealed.

Educated by the nuns of Loreto Convent in Perth, she demanded piano lessons and the convent teachers quickly perceived her gift; both Percy Grainger and Wilhelm Backhaus, on hearing her play, were full of praise and advice. For Grainger she was, quite simply, 'the most transcendentally gifted child he had ever heard', while Backhaus, more practically, suggested that

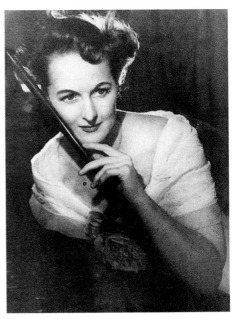

Film-star good looks: 'Ragged Eilee' transformed

she leave Australia and commence serious study in Leipzig. And so it was that after funds had been raised, a characteristically frightened but determined teenager set sail for a deeply alien environment. In Leipzig, where she studied with Robert Teichmüller and Max Pauer, she combined her natural gifts with an iron will to succeed, building a technical foundation and dexterity that would later awe and astonish even the most seasoned audiences during her brief and hectic concert career. There were further periods of study with Adelina de Lara (the last surviving student of Clara Schumann) and Tobias Matthay (whose pupils included Dame Myra Hess, Irene Scharrer and Dame Moura Lympany) in London. In Berlin she also played for Artur Schnabel whom she fondly recalled, in a talk given at the British Institute of Recorded Sound, as a kindly gentleman who took pity on a cold and bemused young girl, offering her a cup of cocoa by way of comfort and solace. But her career was already on course.

A letter of introduction to Sir Henry Wood led to her début in 1930 playing Prokofiev's Third Concerto (an audacious choice for the time) at the Promenade Concerts, where she became a firm favourite, and also the commencement, under fairy-tale circumstances, of her recording career. Anxious to make a 78 disc for her own critical perusal, she saved enough money to pay for the privilege (hardly an instance of vanity recording!) and played Paul de Schlözer's A flat *Etude*, Op. 1 (a fearsomely demanding finger-twister, often used by Rachmaninov for a preliminary flexing of muscles) and Liszt's F minor *Etude* ('La leggierezza'). Her amazed listeners erased her sense of failure, promising the return of her hard-earned money on condition that she record anything she chose from her already extensive repertoire. These, then, were the years of the legendary 1933-42 recordings, reeled off at the rate of a record a month over roughly a ten-year period. Her star shone with increasing brilliance, illuminating a time of dazzling international celebrity, of temperamental fire, flashing fingers and a rare communicative force and ardour.

Rise and fall

Her repertoire became immense and included over 70 works for piano and orchestra, each painstakingly prepared (she was hardly a 'quick study pianist' and, as her scores often show, was inclined to pencil in the names of notes lying above and below the ledger lines). These extended from Mozart through all the major and minor romantics (Tchaikovsky No. 2 as well as No. 1, the Rimsky-Korsakov Concerto, Busoni's *Indianische Fantasie*, and so on) to pioneering fare by John Ireland and Shostakovich. The transformation of

'Ragged Eilee' could hardly have been more complete. A woman of charismatic and arresting beauty, Eileen Joyce gave recital after recital and concerto marathon after concerto marathon, performing in Brazil before calling in at London's Royal Albert Hall for another concert before continuing the following night to Helsinki for further engagements. Later she would exclaim in wonder at her former strength and tenacity ('Chopin 1, Rachmaninov 2, the John Ireland Concerto and Beethoven's *Emperor* all in one evening; I don't know where I got the energy!'). Concertos followed with the Berlin Philharmonic under Celibidache, a sugar-sweet, fantasy biography, *Prelude*, was published by Oxford University Press and there were appearances and soundtrack recordings for such films as *The Seventh Veil* and *Brief Encounter* where many members of the public, musical or otherwise, made their first acquaintance with Rachmaninov's Second Concerto.

However, her capacity audiences, promoters, exploiters and most of all herself failed to realize that she was, after all, human rather than a robot. A sense of disillusion ensued and her private anguish became public while still in her

Eileen Joyce: 'I worked too hard and travelled too much'

forties when she announced the end of her career. In her own words, 'I worked too hard and travelled too much. I felt depleted spiritually and mentally, I was like a shell with nothing inside any more. I had been whipped along by ambition and the desire to project myself and it was too much. I got to hate my own name. You give out so much and nothing comes back. For 25 years I lived totally for my music, there was nothing else in my life.' Suddenly the tenacious desire for a career was countered by a no less determined desire to end it. Her decision came to her in a flash while journeying in a rickshaw between Hong Kong and Kowloon and she later gave her last recital in Scotland in 1962, symbolically closing the piano lid and terminating one of the most brilliant and widely publicized of all musical careers. And having stopped the roundabout she found a novel sense of tranquillity, dispersing her immense energy in a wide variety of pursuits and taking a keen interest in the careers of the more interesting up-and-coming young pianists. The late Terence Judd was among her favourites and she often marvelled at his performance of the Samuel Barber Sonata. For 40 years Eileen Joyce played the piano occasionally and for her own pleasure though she confessed that every night around five o'clock she reached a low ebb, 'because for 25 years that was the time I would be getting ready for my concert. And so every evening the shadow of the tension returns. You see, all my concerts were a matter of life and death for me and the spectre of possible failure returns to haunt me. I've had an odd life. I haven't liked it much.'

'All my concerts were a matter of life and death for me': a photo taken from the cover of a souvenir concert programme

A personal reminiscence

The first concert I ever attended was a recital by Eileen Joyce. Even today I can recall a programme that included Schumann's *Carnaval*, Liszt's First *Mephisto Waltz* and an assortment of shorter works including Schubert's A flat *Impromptu*, D899 No. 4; heady delights for a seven-year-old. The effect of her vibrant artistry and presence was indelible and many years later my visits to her home, first in Chartwell and then in Limpsfield, Surrey, seemed an uncanny form of continuity. There, conversation would bubble and sparkle into life only to end a few minutes later, her initial delight abruptly clouded and coloured by too many sombre memories.

Reminiscing happily about past colleagues ('Whatever happened to old Benno?'), she would sometimes take a sharper line with those who had temporarily incurred her displeasure ('That sort of playing blows away in the wind like so much orange fluff' or 'She was always poking her nose in other people's business. She'd have made an excellent spy,' followed by the afterthought, 'I really was very fond of her.').

Her attitude to my work on her behalf, on the reissue of her recordings, was mixed and she clearly feared any form of attention connected with her former life. She could be teasingly whimsical and elusive when requests were made for her own personal copies of her records (EMI had lost or destroyed many of the original metals), hiding some and conveniently forgetting the whereabouts of others. Attempts to get her to listen to her incomparably subtle and dextrous performance of, say, Grieg's 'Brooklet' (*Lyric Pieces*, Op. 62 No. 1) were met with a

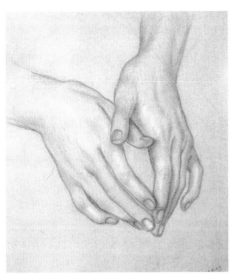

A sketch of Eileen Joyce's hands

concern for her cats' welfare ('Lucy and Daniel don't get on. They fight all the time; isn't it awful?'), and a further attempt to discuss the success of her recordings in America, most notably in Miami, met with complete failure. I might as well have been talking about the Isle of Man. There were occasional threats to destroy what she called her 'past', conjuring a fearful picture of a funeral pyre of records, programmes and memorabilia, most of which were, thankfully, rescued and shipped off to the University of Western Australia in Perth.

In 1991 I felt saddened but privileged when asked to speak at Eileen Joyce's funeral in Limpsfield before a large gathering which testified to her legendary status. It was an opportunity to recall an indomitable and enchanting spirit whose magic lives on, notably in Testament's newly released tribute, contradicting her sad assertion, 'Once you stop playing, you are forgotten.' **IPQ**

disarming diffidence ('Just trickles along, and the sound is so clear'). Further efforts to interest her in her interpretation of Chopin's G minor *Ballade*, Op. 52 were foiled by her sudden

All photos courtesy of Bryce Morrison

....

Review of Eileen Joyce's Parlophone Recordings on page 107

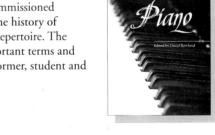

Ravel's Left-Hand Concerto on record

CHARLES HOPKINS APPRAISES THE PERFORMANCE HISTORY OF THIS

BEAUTIFULLY CRAFTED CONCERTO – A WORK WHICH IS TOO OFTEN

OVERSHADOWED BY ITS MORE POPULAR 'TWO-HANDED' SISTER

Ravel once confessed: 'It is by imitating that I innovate.' Later, *par revanche*, as if to put the curious further off the scent, he was to recant by saying that he would rather the next generation detest his works than be too much influenced by them. Even Ravel at his most elliptical, however, could not conceal beneath two such elegant paradoxes that distinctive voice through which his personal search for the means of spiritual catharsis, particularly in his final compositions, may be heard. Indeed, Frederick Goldbeck in *La Revue Musicale* (March 1933) remarks that in his piano music Ravel harked back on the one hand to the classicism of Mozart, or, further, to Couperin, and on the other to Liszt. This has led a number of commentators to the conclusion that in his two piano concertos Ravel was, in effect, in the one cleansing himself of the deep underlying grief so subtly, yet so poignantly, adumbrated in *Le tombeau de Couperin*, while in the other purging the romantic demons he had evoked in *Gaspard de la nuit*. Moreover, this laying of ghosts in the context of formative antecedence may also be seen as complementing Ravel's private search for a means of deliverance from the spectral visions of his own psyche.

The manifold contradictions encountered at every turn in any examination of Ravel the man and Ravel the composer present in their recognition a multiplicity of questions, the solutions to which time and again themselves prove as readily illuminating as the most inscrutable *koan* from the lips of a venerable Zen master. How, for instance, are we to reconcile the extreme

fastidiousness Ravel exhibited in both his music and so many areas of his everyday life, such as the impeccably drawn façade he cultivated from his youth in both dress and manners – surely more consistent with the fashionable *fin de siècle* posture of Baudelaire than merely symptomatic of a need to compensate for his slightness of physique – with what Marguerite Long once described as his 'legendary abstractedness' in other areas? Given his fascination for the precision workmanship of such mechanical devices as clocks, for example, how may we interpret the copious anecdotal evidence of his total disregard of time and persistent lack of punctuality on a daily basis, all the more perplexing in view of the exactitude and sense of proportion he brought to the dramatic and structural elements of his music? His friend and fellow 'Apache', Emile Vuillermoz, writing in *Les Cahiers d'aujourd'hui* in 1922, perhaps summed up the Ravel 'dilemma' most succinctly: 'One sees in him … isolated details that simply do not go together. He is both a child and an old man. Something of no significance will amuse him, yet at the same time his gaunt face often takes on an austere and cold expression. He passes in an instant from the carefree abandon of a child to a world-weary *gravitas*. He often appears as though in pain, his tormented features and deep frown signifying who knows what dark conflict … The look of an anxious young fox or a mouse sensing traps everywhere is peculiar in an artist so lucid, so spontaneous and precise, who has nothing to fear from life. Is he the only one who fails to recognize the infallibility of his own creative powers?'

Ravel was a complex man: extremely fastidious and precise on the one hand, and notoriously unpunctual on the other

Photo AKG London

The origins of the concerto

For a composer who was such a master at writing individually for both the piano and the orchestra – like Stravinsky, Ravel used to orchestrate at the piano, while, in turn, he subsequently orchestrated many of his piano works – it is, perhaps, ironic that he should have embarked on his two concerted works for piano and orchestra so late in his career, even allowing for the special circumstances which gave rise to the Concerto for the Left-Hand. Intriguing, too, that the grandiloquence of the single-movement Left-Hand Concerto should contrast so markedly in range of texture and expression with its companion work, which, although conceived in three movements, creates the impression more of an amplified chamber *divertissement*, a distinction acknowledged by Ravel himself. Indeed, on one level it is possible to see in the sheer sweep and virtuosity of the Left-Hand Concerto an almost defiant dismissal of the gauntlet thrown down by the imposed restrictions. The appeal of such a commission to Ravel was, however, more than simply the self-referential delight of finding a sophisticated intellectual solution to a specific physical limitation, and the outcome was without question the result of an extraordinary outpouring of imaginative intensity rather than the purely cerebral manipulation and rationalizing of a particular set of variables. Equally, the objective clarity Ravel sought and so jealously guarded is ever-present, yet, as with all his most finely-wrought works, never at the expense of creative vitality. Indeed, Vladimir Jankélévich, commenting on the control Ravel so rigorously exercised over his means of expression, even in such apparently improvisatory contexts as the jazzy syncopations of the Left-Hand Concerto, highlights the dangers of confusing stylized precision with an unwillingness to reveal deeper levels of sensibility. By the same token it must be conceded that the sensibilities involved derive in large measure from secondary sources, especially the world of children and the exotic, affording Ravel the objective distance to shield his more personal imaginative impulses from the intrusive gaze of a wider public.

The evident contrariety in Ravel's artistic persona may be illustrated most clearly by the instances of his working simultaneously on more than one composition, each inhabiting a diametrically antithetical emotional world. The *Sonatine* and *Miroirs* of 1904-5 and, especially, *Ma mère l'oye* and *Gaspard de la nuit* of 1908 provide clear instances of this. Indeed, the duality which pervades almost every aspect of the Left-Hand Concerto (on which he was, characteristically, working concurrently with the G major during the period 1929-30) derives in large measure from these last two compositions, both psychologically and in purely technical terms. In alluding to each in turn, Ravel evokes an almost Proustian nostalgia for the lost innocence of childhood and the unaffected purity of its emotional horizons alongside a resourceful transformation and refinement of the type of quintessentially Lisztian virtuosity explored in, for instance, 'Scarbo'. From this position it is but a short step to seeing in the Left-Hand Concerto the ultimate expression of Ravel's fixation with the concept of death, a preoccupation which, as Arbie Orenstein has noted (Dover Publications: 1991), spans his creative output from the *Ballade de la reine morte d'aimer* through 'Le gibet' to 'Aoua' from *Chansons madécasses* – the *Dies irae* outline in the *più vivo* prior to the recapitulation is unmistakable. Although the dramatic power and expressive range of the piece set it apart from its companion, the unexpected portentousness of the writing left some bewildered. Dominique Sordet, for instance, as quoted in Madeleine Goss's biography *Bolero* (Henry Holt: 1940), saw in it only 'the pathetic struggle which had already been declared between [Ravel's] creative intelligence and implacable disease.' Equally, the congruities evident between the concluding passages of *La valse* and the sardonic death-rattle in the final gesture of the Left-Hand Concerto, to which Henri Gil-Marchex refers as a 'ricanement diabolique' (*La Revue Musicale*, December 1938), are no mere coincidence. The physical appearance of the one-armed Viennese pianist Paul Wittgenstein, who commissioned the concerto was, after all, a vivid reminder of the tragic futility of a war in which the composer had himself lost many close friends.

Ravel lavished an unusual amount of care on the concerto, even by his meticulous standards,

> *Although the dramatic power and expressive range of the piece set it apart from its companion, the unexpected portentousness of the writing left some bewildered*

and made a particular study of the *Etudes* for the left-hand, Op. 135 of Saint-Saëns, as well as Godowsky's transcriptions of the *Etudes* of Chopin – the whole layout of Ravel's cadenza bears a clear indebtedness to Godowsky's version of the *Etude* in E flat minor, Op. 10 No. 6. He also examined various works by Czerny, the *Prélude et Nocturne*, Op. 9 by Scriabin, and Alkan's 'Etude pour la main gauche seule', Op. 76 No. 1 – the figuration and tonality of the final bars of Ravel's concerto actually bear an uncanny similarity to the concluding gestures of Alkan's 'Etude pour la main *droite* seule', Op. 76 No. 2! Ravel had undertaken a similarly intense study of the concertos of Mozart and Saint-Saëns during the early stages of his work on the G major Concerto. An indication of the fascination and extreme seriousness with which Ravel approached the task of writing to this unusual specification may be inferred from a communication he made to Michel Calvocoressi, which also appeared in *The Daily Telegraph* as quoted by Roland-Manuel in *A la gloire de Ravel* (Paris: 1938): 'The Concerto … contains many jazz effects, and the writing is not so light [as in the G major]. In a work of this kind it is essential to give the impression of a texture no thinner than that of a part written for both hands. For the same reason I resorted to a style that is much nearer to that of the more solemn kind of traditional concerto.'

Early 'improvements'

Paul Wittgenstein had, of course, already commissioned a substantial number of concerted works during the 1920s from composers such as Rudolf Braun, Paul Hindemith, Erich Korngold, Franz Schmidt, Eduard Schütt, Karl Weigl and, most notably, Richard Strauss. His musical conservatism, however, had led to a good many disagreements with composers of a less reactionary persuasion, a situation from which Ravel himself was not entirely exempt. Wittgenstein himself later admitted that his initial reaction to Ravel's piece had been somewhat muted, to some extent due to Ravel's not

Great Pianists of the Past on PALEXA

COLLECTION DOCUMENTS   **CD-0509**

COLLECTION DOCUMENTS   **CD-0503**

entirely secure two-handed rendition of the solo part, followed by the orchestral score, at a preliminary session in the composer's home. Subsequently, if a little grudgingly, he did acknowledge the greatness of the work – it was to prove a considerable asset to the pianist, who received many glowing reviews of his performances of it – and then only after he had made an appreciable number of 'improvements' to the score, much to Ravel's displeasure. Marguerite Long, in *Au Piano avec Maurice Ravel* (Juilliard: 1971), recalls an especially highly-charged meeting between the two men at a dinner at Wittgenstein's house in Vienna after which the host had given a performance of his retouched version of Ravel's concerto which he had already played in public in the Austrian capital on November 27th, 1931: 'During the performance, I was following with the score ... and was able to observe on Ravel's ever-darkening face the misdeeds of our host's initiatives. As soon as it was finished, Ravel slowly advanced towards Wittgenstein and said to him: "But that is not it at all." And the other defended himself: "I am an old pianist and that doesn't sound!" "I am an old orchestrator and it *does* sound!" replied Ravel.' Ravel's subsequent opposition to Wittgenstein's projected Paris presentation of the work led to the postponement of the performance, which as a result did not take place until January 17th, 1933, ironically under the composer's baton. Wittgenstein had written to him, 'Interpreters do not have to be slaves.' Ravel tersely replied, 'Interpreters *are* slaves!'

With masterly understatement, the conductor Trevor Harvey, who had known Wittgenstein personally, wrote in a tribute in *The Gramophone* (June 1961) that 'the nervous intensity that he developed led him often to play insensitively and loudly and not always with great accuracy.' Such an assessment is amply borne out by the two recorded performances of the Ravel concerto (and, indeed, by his later rendering of the Strauss *Parergon*). Even allowing for the pressures of public performance, the evidence is, I am sad to say, quite frankly

painful, and wholly inconsistent with the lavish praise bestowed on Wittgenstein by normally discerning critics who were apt to comment at the time on his capacity for 'miraculously transforming his left-hand into two, one singing, the other accompanying.' In the event none of the work's subtleties are explored, much less any suggestion of a singing tone; and the crude assault to which the music is subjected probably tells us more about the understandable frustrations of the performer than it does about the piece – even those moments where the writing does evoke a mood of savagery are coarsened to the point of grotesquerie. In a sense, however, the all-too-obvious shortcomings in Wittgenstein's performances are of secondary importance to his personal courage and the dogged pursuit of an improbable career against all odds.

Miscalculation versus dignity

If Wittgenstein's recorded performances, for all their historical significance, fall into the category of 'heroic failures', it is, regrettably, less easy to view **Alfred Cortot**'s version in quite so charitable a light. Throughout, tempos appear at best arbitrary, and often too fast for any degree of accuracy or articulation. Similarly, pedalling would seem to have been decided upon

Alfred Cortot: a highly individual, even quirky performance *Photo EMI*

on a purely *ad hoc* basis, and even Cortot's legendary *cantabile* is conspicuous by its absence, melodic lines not infrequently being reduced to a succession of barely related pitches, stabbed at in isolation by the pianist's overtaxed thumb. Curiously, the rhetorical aspects of the writing, in which one might have expected Cortot to shine, find him on this occasion under acute strain, inner harmonies of chords scarcely an approximation, explicit pedal effects completely misconstrued or totally ignored, the whole displaying an underlying instability at odds with the heroic grandeur of the music. The final cadenza is likewise reduced to a generalized blur, dynamic shadings disappearing under a welter of inaccuracy and inappropriate gesture, robbing the music of all sense of organic growth. In the face of such palpable desperation the dubious merits of Cortot's two-handed version might well appear to have been a viable alternative option, but that is hardly the point. In mitigation, it perhaps says a good deal about the force of Cortot's personality that he could persuade Munch to collude with such perversity.

By contrast, **Jacques Février**'s two performances are models of dignified restraint as well as consistency. Ravel himself found in Février a sympathetic and highly competent executant, selecting him to become the first French interpreter of the work after the expiry of Wittgenstein's six-year exclusive rights over the piece – Ravel considered Février's performance, on March 19th, 1937, to have been the work's authentic première. As, in effect, the concerto's official ambassador (the composer had coached him in great detail) Février performed it in Boston in November 1937 under Koussevitzky to wide critical acclaim. In both recordings Février opts for a measured approach, the bravura of the opening solo being tempered by a degree of circumspection, the final *glissando* emerging as a broad brush stroke rather than the familiar vulgar expedient to which it is so often reduced. Février's tempos likewise studiously avoid extremes, allowing the music to evolve without recourse to obtrusive agogic exaggerations, sectional transitions occurring smoothly and with an inevitability which nevertheless does not preclude contrasts of characterization. In the jazz-style episodes he chooses a brisk tempo in the second recording, pushing ahead at the expense of precise ensemble, but everywhere there is a sense of unforced expression, not

lacking in colour or vitality but subtly compelling, despite the absence of superficial heroics.

There is a consistency and finish, too, about the two **Jacqueline Blancard** performances, the earlier of which was, in fact, the first studio recording of the piece. In 1929, at the age of 20, Blancard had played *Ma mère l'oye* with the composer in Geneva and certainly those aspects of the concerto which hark back to the enchanted world of the Empress of the Pagodas are especially affecting. In both versions, however, there is an underplaying of the grander gestural elements of the writing which creates the impression of dramatic opportunities missed and many of the darker recesses of the work's inner world studiously unexplored. Curiously, as if to lighten the texture from the outset, Blancard, in the first version, elects to play the first octave of her opening solo, in fact, an octave higher than written – Février adopts a similar ploy before the *strepitoso* descent prior to the second orchestral entry. Whatever reservations one might have about Blancard's readings, they nevertheless display a concern for rhythmic accuracy and clear articulation, firmness of attack without overemphasis, and an impressive degree of integration with the orchestra, which exemplify the teaching of her mentor Isidor Philipp at its best: 'Play fast, but never so fast that a note does not have the time to say its name in passing.' Likewise, dynamic extremes are consciously scaled down, although the approach to the orchestral re-entry at the end of the cadenza is beautifully proportioned.

Variety within a French tradition

If Blancard's versions concentrate on extreme limpidity of texture and the nostalgic vision of lost innocence, the various performances by **Robert Casadesus** focus more on the dramatic and structural aspects of the music with particular emphasis on the importance of integrated tempo relationships. Casadesus had played *Gaspard de la nuit* to the composer as early as 1922, becoming in 1924 the first pianist to give an all-Ravel recital, and he and Ravel regularly appeared together throughout the decade. By the time he first recorded the Left-Hand Concerto in 1947 Casadesus had already been performing it on both sides of the Atlantic for ten years, and his conception of the work was

Concerto (Odyssey ⊙ Y35216) surely deserves reissue.

A rational approach to tempo relationships is also strongly evident in the performance of **Vlado Perlemuter**, a reflection once again of the personal influence of the composer. Perlemuter, in fact, did not have the opportunity to see Ravel after 1929, the year in which he performed the complete solo works in two recitals, having studied them with the composer.

Robert Casadesus's masterly playing reveals his thorough conception of the work

firmly established. Indeed, one might say that Casadesus's view of the work looks forward in its concentration on a rhetorical projection and the turbulent drama of the writing to a more contemporary style, which in lesser hands can be seen to contribute to a feeling of homogenized uniformity in later versions. In its combination of clarity and articulation, along with a deeper touch than the purely digital style that typified the old French School, Casadesus's playing embodied an eclectic ideal which transcended the confines of national boundaries. Equally, the apparent directness of his playing, which exudes scrupulous integrity and utter conviction, draws the listener in through its sheer power of concentration and clear sense of purpose. Although the range of colour and dynamic subtlety Casadesus employs in the concerto may not be as wide as that in his recordings of *Miroirs* or parts of *Gaspard*, the clarity and honesty of the playing is most persuasive – in the first version there is a momentary loss of composure in the *Allegro* which is left unaltered – while the physical mastery of the most extreme demands, if not infallible, reminds us of his formidable command of a Lisztian idiom – his recording of the A major

The interpretative ideals inculcated through Ravel's coaching in the solo *oeuvre* are, however, clearly carried through to his conception of the concerto. Textual fidelity combined with precise tonal definition mark out Perlemuter's performance, along with a subtle and masterly application of a wide diversity of pedal techniques which effect clarity without dryness and a full tonal palette with barely any concession to harmonic overlapping. In this respect Perlemuter appears to find a more satisfactory solution than Casadesus, achieving the joint objectives of greater clarity as well as greater warmth. Perlemuter also achieves an unusually stable equilibrium between rhythmic vitality and agogic control in the *Allegro*, where the thematic transformation of the initial horn motif emerges with appropriate intensity and minatory weight yet without any loss of momentum. Perlemuter's version, for all the lacklustre orchestral playing, is certainly one of the most satisfying of the earlier recordings, striking a rare balance between conflicting elements within the music and amply justifying his patrician status in this repertoire.

Vlado Perlemuter: his colourful and concise interpretation testifies to his high reputation in this repertoire

Two more of the finest recordings, also from the late 1950s, are those of Jean Casadesus and Samson

Samson François's account is typically imaginative and rhapsodic *Photo EMI*

Chopin No. 2 and Liszt No. 1 in one evening with the same forces as in his recording. He was notoriously variable in the recording studio and we should be thankful that he was 'in the mood' on this occasion to recapture some of the excitement of that evening. Throughout one is made to see performance as re-creation rather than mere repetition. That both Jean Casadesus and Samson François should have died with so much still to do serves as a poignant reminder of Plautus's warning: *quem di diligunt adolescens moritur* ('Whom the gods love dies young').

The Americans factors

Two highly impressive versions by American-born pianists, **John Browning** and **Julius Katchen**, also deserve mention, for one his first concerto recording, for the other his last. Each brings an arresting power and authority to the piece, Browning in particular producing a telling combination of control and élan, especially in the larger-scale rhetorical writing of the first solo and the cadenza. Katchen, likewise, brings a commanding virtuosity to those passages, especially with his opening salvo – his account of the Britten *Diversions*, another work written for Wittgenstein, is similarly memorable – although tempos overall seem less well assimilated into the unified whole. Not surprisingly, each is also especially effective in the jazz references of the *Allegro* – one recalls outstanding Gershwin performances from both artists. Perhaps, though, Browning's realization of the darker aspects of the piece is the more sombre, more austere, more redolent of the twilight world of *Gaspard*, a work he subsequently recorded to impressive effect (RCA ⊙ LSC3028).

François, each in its own way making a highly persuasive case for the work. **Jean Casadesus**'s reading is absolutely assured, the most taxing extended passagework delivered with a controlled clarity and sheer *sangfroid* which contribute to a remarkable extent to the chilling aura of his realization and underpin the pervasive menace of the work's subtextual programme. The dark-hued cadenza, in particular, after emerging *de profundis* from the stygian murk of the *contrabassi*, builds to a terrifying climax with a remorseless cumulative power that has nothing to do with exaggerated effect. **Samson François**, on the other hand, is typically mercurial and unpredictable, yet achieves results no less compelling. Where Casadesus *fils* epitomizes calculation and control, François is all temperament and spontaneity; where the former instils fear with an unswerving sense of direction, the latter will often drop virtually out of sight, only to re-emerge unexpectedly, sweeping all before him. From the outset it is clear that this is not a conventional reading, yet one is no less gripped by the rhapsodic improvisatory licence of his treatment of the *Sarabande* than by other more supposedly disciplined versions – even what one can only assume to be a spectacular misreading prior to the *vivo* sequence does not faze him (or us!), nor does it interrupt the torrential imaginative flow. Equally, the *più vivo ed accelerando* which precedes the recapitulation is, for once, observed, its *Dies irae* allusions hurtling past in a blaze of virtuosity towards an inevitable nemesis. Astonishingly, François performed the concerto along with Bartók No. 3,

Just as Casadesus *père* arguably enjoyed higher regard in the United States than in his native France, Katchen's reputation was greater outside North America. In the last years of his life he lived in Paris, where one of his protégés was the young **Pascal Rogé**, whose recordings of

Pascal Rogé: a polished performance *Photo Decca*

Jaques Samuel
P I A N O S

Winner of the *Best Retailer of the Year 1996 - MIA*

C. BECHSTEIN

Bösendorfer

STEINWAY & SONS

Jaques Samuel Pianos is the principal supplier in the U.K. for Bechstein and Bösendorfer pianos and we also offer Steinway pianos lovingly restored to the highest standards using the finest German materials

- -

For Further information please return this coupon to Bechstein House

☐ *Bechstein Pianos*	*Name*
☐ *Bösendorfer Pianos*	*School or Institution*
☐ *Steinway Pianos*	*Address*
☐ *Hire/Tuning Services*	
☐ *Refurbishment Services*	
☐ *Forthcoming Events*	*Telephone Number*

Ravel's complete solo works, made when he was in his early twenties, still command the highest respect. His reading of the Left-Hand Concerto is similarly polished and idiomatic in its clarity and textual accuracy. If it lacks the assertive power of some other versions, compensation in plenty may be had from the crystalline textures of those passages whose indebtedness to the spirit of *Ma mère l'oye* is so affecting.

Another pianist with impressive credentials in Ravel was **Werner Haas**, a pupil of Gieseking, whose performance of the concerto is another which achieves a fine balance between brilliance and sensuousness, while exhibiting a good deal of flair for the jazzy parody of the opening in the *Allegro* – he, too, made successful recordings of Gershwin. In fact, alongside Haas, **Hervé Billaut**'s performance with the same orchestra appears almost pedestrian by comparison. Ultimately, however, while the surface effect of Haas's playing is eminently satisfactory, the inner turbulence of the work is underplayed and one is left with an impression more of efficiency than enquiry. At least he has more to say than **Daniel Wayenberg** in an account taken from a public performance in the Concertgebouw. Once again, although it is efficient it reveals little new about the work, and despite some well-defined articulation in the exchanges of the *Allegro*, the playing from both soloist and orchestra is notably short on idiom, seldom rising above the routine.

Finely balanced playing from **Werner Haas** *Photo Philips*

Three notable Russians

A public performance which commands greater interest, however, is that of **Sviatoslav Richter**, given, remarkably and quite literally as an encore immediately after another performance of the piece. The cross-referencing of aspects of both French and Russian culture provides a fascinating alternative gloss on the now-familiar characterizations of structural elements within the music. There is a granitic force about the performance, an inexorable power that is light years away from the finely-drawn lines we have come to expect in Ravel. Richter's reading of the concerto is, in its own way, undeniably impressive (as, indeed, was his vigorous treatment of *Miroirs*), even if the results are hardly endearing. The orientalism in sections of the *Allegro*, for instance, is here projected with almost as much dynamic intensity as the barbaric dance with which it should provide a contrast. Moreover, Richter's view of the work, which he had first studied many years before after injuring a right-hand finger in a fracas in a Moscow bar, would not appear on this occasion inconsistent with his overall conception, as was borne out by a 1983 performance with Barenboim and the Orchestre de Paris. And, as Piero Rattalino observed, the ending of the whole performance is of such brutality that it conveys more the impression of the death of Attila on his wedding night with Ildico than the ironic laugh of the devil.

The versions by **Dmitri Bashkirov** and **Andrei Gavrilov** are far less controversial yet both are highly accomplished. Each appears more

Sviatoslav Richter is undeniably impressive *Photo Decca*

concerned with the dramatic than the sensuous aspects of the writing, although neither is insensitive to the fundamental contrasts inherent within the music. Bashkirov, a prize-winner at the 1955 Marguerite Long-Jacques Thibaud Competition, has since given classes at the Paris Conservatoire, and the resulting exposure of a younger generation of French pianists to Russian pianism in general has broadened their outlook considerably, particularly with respect to tone production and depth of touch. Bashkirov's Left-Hand Concerto is especially impressive in those passages where melody needs to be separated from an extremely active texture, such as in the cadenza where this clarity cannot be achieved at the expense of important subsidiary elements. Indeed, the sheer control of Bashkirov's performance and his complete mastery of both technique and idiom make it one of the finest versions of all. Likewise, Gavrilov's athleticism is particularly effective in areas of rapid lateral displacement, while, almost unexpectedly, the *spiccato* writing of the bridge leading to the *Allegro* is expertly pointed and sufficiently unobtrusive to allow orchestral detail to speak with clarity – a 1968 Bavarian Radio performance by John Ogdon was also notable for a similar response to orchestral colour.

beginnings via some melting passagework to an imposing climax. The performances of two of his students, **Jean-Philippe Collard** and **Michel Béroff**, establish a benchmark of authority on modern renditions of the work. Collard, in particular, has the measure of this music without taking any aspect for granted, and if his juxtaposition of the polarities is just a shade more responsive, Béroff's virtuosity in the declamatory writing is formidably impressive. Collard, too, brings an imposing grandeur to the opening, its bravura, however, appearing more as a vehicle for dark foreboding than display, while the parodied innocence represented by oriental allusions in the *Allegro* is offset most effectively by the percussive rhythms of the devil's dance. The precision of both Collard and Béroff is truly remarkable, every note speaking with clarity while balanced within the whole

Michel Béroff: formidable virtuosity *Photo Cabrol*

Teachers and pupils

Eclectic influences have also affected an older generation of performers and teachers, such as **Pierre Sancan**, whose whole physiological approach was at odds with the predominantly digital technique which runs through the teach-·ings of Marguerite Long. Another well-known teacher, **Jean Doyen**, offers a rather generalized view of the Left-Hand Concerto, with little in the way of dynamic breadth and a marked lack of rhythmic suppleness. To Sancan, however, the piano represented an orchestra whose colouristic potential could only be realized by a full use of the upper arm, shoulder and, indeed, torso. His own *Caprice romantique* for the left-hand demonstrates his understanding of the potential of sinistromanual pianism and his reading of the concerto is thoroughly considered and alive to the multiple inferences that may be drawn from its rapid shifts of mood – his final cadenza is impressively built from its crepuscular

Jean-Phillipe Collard's performance combines precision and intensity *Photo Tennant Artists/Berthelot*

textural framework. Collard, especially, brings a controlled intensity to the apocalyptic *dénouement* towards which he has been leading us with a logical inevitability that has seldom been equalled, much less surpassed.

Another Sancan student, **Abdel Rahman el Bacha**, is less compelling though not appreciably less accomplished. He is simply insufficiently varied in his response to textual possibilities and structural components. The same, unfortunately, must be said of **Kun Woo Paik** and **Georges Pludermacher**. Paik in particular, falls into the trap of poorly delineated tempo relationships, with the result that there is little sense of organic growth, despite his attempts at assertiveness at the first piano entry, although throughout he is not helped by especially sluggish orchestral support. The lack of an integrated approach to tempo also mars **Thiollier**'s otherwise workable account of the piece, the *Allegro* devoid of rhythmic bite and any genuine sense of menace at the tempo chosen.

Cécile Ousset: a powerful and distinguished display

Efficiency without depth

Nor, unfortunately, despite an enviable command of the sheer physical demands of the music, do either of **François-René Duchâble**'s performances give even a fleeting glimpse of Ravel's kaleidoscopic necromancy. Everywhere one is made aware of the finish and ease of Duchâble's technique, and there is never any danger that, even when the music is at its most cruelly demanding, anything might occur to disturb the controlled surface image. While impressive in one sense, then, a suspicion of glibness, of disengagement, pervades the performances which leaves one longing, say, for the abandon of François or the insight of Collard.

The same lack of involvement is a feature of **Aldo Ciccolini**'s eminently accomplished account. This is not to suggest that Ciccolini fails to recognize the sombre presentiment concealed within the music, but that his polished pianistic effects seem seldom to penetrate far beneath the surface. Indeed, nor does **Jean-Yves**

Thibaudet's version by comparison with his recordings of the complete solo works: the potential afforded by his controlled dexterity is never quite realized and even the cadenza passes by without coming close to catching fire. It is a shame, too, not to be able to view **Zoltán Kocsis**'s performance more favourably, but again here is a remarkable virtuoso who appears on this occasion to be inhibited by his technical reserves rather than liberated by them to explore dimensions of the text beneath the bravura exterior. Curiously, the opening solo is unexpectedly subdued, and although the final cadenza is predictably assured, one's suspicions of what may lie over the abyss are never truly addressed. In passing, the exploration of a number of extraneous instrumental effects, presumably to underline the jazzy elements of the writing, is especially ill-conceived, is of extremely questionable taste, and runs the risk of trivializing the sinister machinations afoot. Ravel needs no such special pleading.

If the demands of the writing appear almost too strenuous for **Yukie Nagai**, the same charge cannot be levelled against **Cécile Ousset** whose account is distinguished without offering any specific insights. Nevertheless, her muscularity in the opening cadenza makes a powerful case for the music, while the second subject emerges with an expressive tenderness that one frequently misses in other performances. Arguably, though, she is most successful in building and sustaining an ominous tension throughout the diabolical dance, whose grotesque contortions of earlier thematic motifs are projected with an energetic force that is highly arresting. Less vividly characterized are the performances of **Alicia de Larrocha**, yet the implicit Hispanicism of the *Sarabande* is captured with an appropriately idiomatic sombreness, evoking the supernatural vision of Merimée's Gallic view of Spain with a rare acuity. Beside Larrocha's timbral perspicacity, **Monique Haas**'s version seems somewhat lightweight, even though she was closely associated with the concerto, which she performed along with Mozart's K466 for her

New York début in 1960. Despite the undeniable charm and clarity of her playing, in the end one misses an element of breadth in her reading, an element which is also lacking in **Anne Quéffelec**'s otherwise alert, if small-scaled, version. On the other hand, **Hanae Nakajima** presents an account that is more worthy than inspired, addressing many of the issues but with insufficient characterization to provide lasting satisfaction, much less enlightenment. It is worth mentioning that, given her limited span, the solutions Larrocha finds to problematic chordal extensions and wide-spaced passagework are invariably highly ingenious and are an example to many whose compromises are rhythmically ungainly and are apt to obscure melodic contours which require firm delineation.

If **Boris Krajný** and **Federico Osorio** display a measure of flair and authority in largely familiar presentations of the material and **Fowke** worthily claims the middle ground in a competent but otherwise unexceptional performance, it is sad that **Michele Campanella**'s recording is quite so earnest and earthbound, given his obviously high degree of technical competence. Sad, too, that the only recording by so eminent and experienced an artist as **Abbey Simon** appears to have been made in greater haste than desirable, both for practical considerations of ensemble and for any measure of interpretative depth.

Left-hand specialists

Like Wittgenstein, **Siegfried Rapp** was a casualty of war who determinedly continued a career, achieving a considerable reputation in left-hand repertoire. His performance of the concerto, unlike that of Wittgenstein, is assured without being exceptional, although there is some authority in the playing which raises it above the commonplace. A more imposing pianist, however, who for some time suffered a nervous problem which precluded him from using his right hand, and both of whose two recordings of the concerto command respect, is **Leon Fleisher**. (A recording from Gary Graffman, who suffered a similar injury, is surely overdue.) The later of Fleisher's two recordings, in particular, has a hugely impressive sweep and an intense austerity which, while focusing on one specific element of the equation, none the less conveys an appropriate impression

of dark presentiment. Although perhaps not as unassailably fluent as Rogé, Collard or Béroff, nor as inspirational as François, Fleisher's is a grandiose conception which commands the greatest respect, if not necessarily love.

Final thoughts

Another front-runner, despite a number of highly personal responses which some might view as mannered, is **Louis Lortie**. Even though tempos appear more in isolation than as a part of proportioned overall strategy, even though rubatos can seem at times to stretch the bounds of rhetorical latitude, and even though, particularly in the closing section, ensemble is not

Leon Fleisher's two recordings of the work are both held in high regard *Photo Sony Classical*

always as tight as it needs to be, there is an idiosyncratic sumptuousness about this performance which makes it unusually compelling. A version which displays no such self-indulgence, but finds truth in logic and proportion is that of **Krystian Zimerman**. Without self-conscious mock-heroics and without recourse to extremes, Zimerman's performance (conducted by Pierre Boulez) is one of the most remarkably 'finished' readings of all. The degree of calculation, the precise structural geometry and rigorous control of all physical aspects of the performance – witness the pedalling leading into the *Sarabande* in the first piano entry – can at times, however,

A remarkably 'finished' recording from Krystian Zimerman *Photo DG/Susesch Bayat*

leave the overall impression of a performance that is in some respects unequal to the sum of its very considerable parts, so perfectly self-contained does each element appear. Compared with Boulez's other recording of the work, a highly creditable version with **Philippe Entremont**, who stresses the widest contrasts of mood and whose performance, as such, is successful within the context of its own frame of reference, the orchestral playing is likewise of an altogether different level of attainment. Such discipline and control down to the last fraction of a point may seem to rob the music of its lifeforce of spontaneity, to whatever degree that may be applied. Equally, though, it may represent a new direction for the work to explore, in the same way that the impact of wider stylistic miscegenation has been seen to lead to a more empirical approach independent of national lines of demarcation.

Even after listening to more than 50 individual recordings of the Left-Hand Concerto, that it should maintain its fascination for me is an indication of the multiplex possibilities still to be explored in the work. There are artists whom one would like to have heard in the piece, such as Gieseking and Curzon, and there are those who have yet to commit their thoughts to disc, such as the Canadian left-hand specialist, Raoul Sosa, whose resourceful transcription of *La valse* is both inventive and idiomatic; Sigurd Slåttebrekk's *Gaspard* also makes one wonder what insights he might bring to the concerto. For the time being, however, we may consider ourselves fortunate to have access not only to the achievements of Bashkirov, Browning and Fleisher, but especially those of Février and Perlemuter, Casadesus, *père et fils*, François, Rogé, Béroff, Collard and now Zimerman.[IPQ]

RAVEL'S LEFT-HAND PIANO CONCERTO: THE DISCOGRAPHY

Compiled by Donald Manildi; Charles Hopkins's recommendations are printed in bold

Date	Pianist	Orchestra & conductor	Record company & number
20/2/37*	Wittgenstein	Concertgebouw / Walter	Memories ① GM3009/10
1938	Blancard	Paris Phil Soc / Munch	Dante ① LYS270
1939	Cortot	Paris Conservatoire Orch / Munch	Pearl ① GEMMCD9491
1942	**Février**	**Paris Conservatoire Orch / Munch**	**Dante ① LSY270**
1947	R. Casadesus	Philadelphia / Ormandy	Sony Classical ① MH2K63316
1952*	R. Casadesus	Vienna SO / Celibidache	Enterprise ① LV946/7
1952	Blancard	Suisse Romande Orch / Ansermet	London ① LL797
c1954	Doyen	Lamoureux Orch / Fournet	Epic ◉ LC3123
1955	**Perlemuter**	**Colonne Concerts SO / Horenstein**	**Vox ① CDX2 5507**
1957	**J. Casadesus**	**Paris Conservatoire Orch / Dervaux**	**EMI ① CZS5 69467-2**
1957	**Février**	**French Rad Nat Orch / Tzipine**	**EMI ① CZS5 69464-2**
1957	Wittgenstein	Metropolitan Op Orch / Rudolf	Period ◉ 742
1959	**François**	**Paris Cons Orch / Cluytens**	**EMI ① CDC7 47368-2**
1960	**Browning**	**Philharmonia / Leinsdorf**	**EMI ① CDM5 65923-2**
1960	**R. Casadesus**	**Philadelphia / Ormandy**	**American Columbia ◉ MS6272**
1965	M. Haas	Orch Nat de Paris / Paray	DG ① 439 666-2GX2
c1965	Bashkirov	Moscow PO / Dubrovsky	Melodiya ◉ S01067/8
1968	W. Haas	Monte Carlo Orch / Galliera	Philips ① 438 353-2PM2
1968	Katchen	LSO / Kertész	Decca ◉ SXL6411
6/6/69*	Richter	Genova Teatro SO / Muti	Stradivarius ① 10024/6
1970	Rapp	Dresden PO / Masur	Berlin Classics ① 0091582BC
c1970	Sancan	Südwestfunk Orch / Dervaux ⹁	Musidisc ◉ 4CRC30
1972	Larrocha	LPO / Foster	Decca ◉ SXL6680
1972	Entremont	Cleveland Orch / Boulez	Sony Classical ① SBK46338
1974	Ciccolini	Orch de Paris / Martinon	EMI ① CDM7 69568-2
1975	Simon	Luxembourg RSO / Froment	Vox ① CDX5032
1975	C. Kahn	LSO / Tzipine	Epidaure ◉ 110005
c1976	Nakajima	Nuremberg SO / Neidlinger	Colosseum ◉ SM610
1976	Queffélec	Strasbourg PO / Lombard	Erato ① 2292-45086-2
1977	Gavrilov	LSO / Rattle	EMI ① CDM7 69026-2
1/3/79*	Wayenberg	Concertgebouw / Kondrashin	Philips ① 412 072-2PM
1979	**Collard**	**Orch Nat de France / Maazel**	**EMI ① CDC7 47386-2**
c1980	Torma	Budapest PO / Pál	Hungaroton ◉ SLPX11789
1981	Paik	Stuttgart RSO / Bertini	Orfeo ① C013821A
1982	**Rogé**	**Montreal SO / Dutoit**	**Decca ① 410 230-2DH**
1982	Fleisher	Baltimore SO / Comissiona	Philips ① 456 775-2PM2
1984	El Bacha	LoirePO / Soustrot	Forlane ① FRL16522
1984	Krajný	Prague SO / Bělohlávek	Supraphon ① 33CO-1717
1985	Osorio	RPO / Bátiz	ASV ① CDQS6092
1986	Duchâble	SRO / Jordan	Erato ① 4509-95902-2
1987	**Béroff**	**LSO / Abbado**	**DG ① 423 665-2GH**
1988	Fowke	LPO / Baudo	CFP ① CD-CFP4667
1989	Campanella	Stuttgart RSO / Gelmetti	EMI ① CDC7 54809-2
1989	Lortie	LSO / Frühbeck de Burgos	Chandos ① CHAN8773
c1990	Achatz	Milan SO / Ferré	EPM ① 982 372
c1990	Billaut	Monte Carlo PO / Bardon	REM ① 311 031
c1990	Jordão	MIT SO / Epstein	MP Classics ① 3-11014
1990	Ousset	CBSO / Rattle	EMI ① CDC7 54158-2
1991	Nagai	Malmö SO / Hirokami	BIS ① CD666
1991	Larrocha	St Louis Orch / Slatkin	RCA ① 09026 60985-2
1991	**Fleisher**	**Boston SO / Ozawa**	**Sony Classical ① SK47188**
1992	Pludermacher	Lille Nat Orch / J-C. Casadesus	Harmonia Mundi ① HMT790 1434
1993	Thiollier	Polish Nat RSO / Wit	Naxos ① 8 550753
1995	Duchâble	Orch de Toulouse / Plasson	EMI ① CDC5 55586-2
1995	Thibaudet	Montreal SO / Dutoit	Decca ① 452 448-2DH
1996	Kocsis	Budapest Festival Orch / I. Fischer	Philips ① 446 713-2PH
1996	**Zimerman**	**LSO / Boulez**	**DG ① 449 231-2GH**
30/10/98*	Block	Sinfonia da Camera / Hobson	Zephyr ① Z11499

Notes

Dates followed by * denote live recording

The lost legend of Cairo

HOROWITZ REFERRED TO IGNACE TIEGERMAN AS THE ONLY RIVAL HE

FEARED: **ALLAN EVANS** TELLS THE STORY OF THIS ELUSIVE PIANIST

AND HIS 16-YEAR QUEST TO TRACK DOWN HIS RECORDED LEGACY

It all happened unexpectedly in the Italian Dolomite mountain village of Siusi in 1981 while undertaking research for a biography of Ignaz Friedman (1882-1948). I had located Lydia Walder (1910-97), his only child, who was spending the summer in her father's mountain villa. The house had been kept intact, containing trunks filled with scores and correspondence. 'Do you know of Tiegerman?' she asked. 'Papa said he was the greatest talent he ever worked with. He lived in Cairo.'

Archives, discographies and private collections failed to provide a single recording by him. German music magazines published between the two world wars (*Neue Zeitschrift für Musik* and *Die Musik*) mentioned concerts by a 'young-blooded Pole, pupil of Friedman' possessing a masterly technique who played with 'an emotional violence'. In a magazine article on his youth in Cairo for *House and Garden* (April 1987), the noted literary scholar and author, Edward Said, recalled his piano teacher, Tiegerman. In private, Said spoke of later studies in New York and Boston with five eminent pedagogues, 'all of whom, rolled into one, would not equal Tiegerman's pinky.'

Australia, 1988: While I was interviewing 16 of Friedman's pupils, one elderly pianist and acquaintance of Godowsky's remembered Friedman, while her daughter mentioned a friend in the United States who had studied with Tiegerman.

I interviewed Nevine Miller, daughter of King Farouk's Prime Minister, who described Tiegerman as resembling both Vladimir Horowitz and Chopin, very short and thin, hardly five-feet tall. She later left Egypt for Paris

in 1948 to study with Marguerite Long, who premièred Ravel's Concerto in G and had had coaching from Debussy and Fauré: after Tiegerman, Mme Long proved disappointing.

An intriguing artist and teacher had vanished, his name absent from all the reference books. Yet Friedman's praise and his pupils' awe led one to suspect that the legacy of an important artist had all but disappeared. On a trip to Egypt in 1993, Said located a tape of Tiegerman and marvelled over his pianism – but became ill before he had the opportunity to copy the recording.

Soon afterwards I produced a CD of Severin Eisenberger, a Polish pianist from Podgorze (a suburb of Kraków), home town of his colleague and friend Ignaz Friedman, as well as of Josef Hofmann. His daughter, Agnes Eisenberger, a prominent music manager, found autograph manuscripts given to her father: among them a *Rêverie Viennoise* by Tiegerman, dedicated to Eisenberger in New York in 1928 when Tiegerman made his only trip to the United States, as accompanist to the violinist Zlatko Balokovic.

During the summer of 1994 I found myself in Milan where I mentioned Tiegerman to Marco Contini, producer of the MC label and collaborator on a series of biographies and CDs devoted to historic Italian conductors. Contini recalled the many Egyptian exiles arriving in Milan in 1956, among them a conductor by the name of Oreste Campisi who once visited the Continis and had left a tape which appeared after a brief search. 'I've never listened to it. Campisi died a few years back. Let's put it on.' Pencilled on the label was 'Brahms – Second Piano Concerto'. In French, an announcer stated that the soloist was Ignace Tiegerman.

Ignace Tiegerman: a fearsome taskmaster

A mystery resolved

The Tiegerman Conservatory was established in Cairo in 1931, on Rue Champollion, near the Cairo Museum. Among the staff were assistants and instructors in theory, violin and voice. Each year, Tiegerman brought teachers over from the Warsaw Conservatory and London's Royal College of Music to examine his students. His standards were such that a certificate from Tiegerman's Conservatory was deemed equivalent to one from the London or Warsaw institutions. A demanding but ingenious teacher, Tiegerman furthered the pedagogy of his teachers Friedman and Leschetizky. Several students recalled detailed advice he gave on technique and musical matters, displaying a subtlety and practical mastery that made difficult works accessible and inspiring for his pupils. It was only during a research trip to Cairo in 1997 that Tiegerman's achievements and the reasons underlying his obscurity finally emerged.

In 1903, at the age of 10, Tiegerman had left his native city of Drohobycz, Poland to study with Leschetizky in Vienna. Along with Mieczyslaw Horszowski he was among the youngest pupils Leschetizky had ever accepted, and he was assigned to Ignaz Friedman, then Leschetizky's assistant. Friedman's instruction continued after Tiegerman made his début in Vienna in 1908 at the age of 15: when Friedman moved to Berlin the following year, Tiegerman joined him and remained in close contact. He studied philosophy at a Berlin university and perfected his cookery skills, becoming a Cordon Bleu chef! Little else is known of his following 20 years in Europe aside from a few surviving concert programmes and reviews of tours in Germany, Austria and Scandinavia. Excessive modesty made him scold listeners who greeted him backstage as 'Maestro': 'I am no Maestro, only a pianist and nothing more. Since I was a child the only thing I wanted to do was to play the piano well.'

Two friends and former pupils in Cairo, Prince Hassan Aziz Hassan and Jaida Hassanein, corroborated that Tiegerman and Vladimir Horowitz had been close friends in Berlin during the 1920s. Unbeknown to Tiegerman, Horowitz privately referred to him as the only rival who could have surpassed him, a rival whom he feared.

Only the first two movements were preserved. Campisi's conducting was masterly, boldly incisive and in perfect harmony with Tiegerman's conception. The sensitivity of the latter's pianism emerged, as did a compelling urgency. One pupil of Tiegerman's noted that he knew no limits in expressivity, always encouraging one to venture as far as possible musically and emotionally. The Brahms demonstrated that Tiegerman had fully inherited Friedman's musical culture, for his playing of the concerto became more than an interpretation, rather a rebirth of the work.

Back in New York, Said mentioned that Henri Barda, a Paris-based pianist and possibly Tiegerman's finest pupil, was performing at Columbia University. In a Chopin group, he played the *Barcarolle* with grandeur, attaining a monumentality which carried through to the end of his programme. Barda acknowledged that his musical language came from Tiegerman, though unfortunately his playing is thus far documented on only three CDs.

On a trip to Austria in 1963, Barda had taken photos of Tiegerman in Kitzbühel – among the few extant photos of him – where his teacher spent his vacations: 'His eyes, they would cut right through you like knives!' Tiegerman's friend, the pianist Stefan Askenase, was also visiting. Barda recalled Tiegerman's tyrannical rages when a pupil was less than prepared at a lesson: often his studio door would swing open, the music would fly out first, followed by the student.

Tiegerman's teachers: Theodor Leschetizky (front row, left) with Ignaz Friedman (front row, right)

along with solo works by Beethoven, Brahms, Fauré and Chopin and his own *Rêverie Viennoise*. Dr Samir Kamel, a pupil (now a physician in Kuwait), made these recordings and once permitted Yassa to make copies before the Gulf's climate nearly destroyed them. The same genius of conception in Tiegerman's Brahms extended to the other composers he performed. At last, a better source of Said's material was found and made accessible.

Two hours of Tiegerman's playing now survives. Yassa noted: 'After hearing him, a piece is spoiled for good. You cannot listen to anyone else play the same work. They do not compare with Tiegerman.'

The Hungerford connection

The late Bruce Hungerford, pianist and Egyptologist, had arrived in Cairo in 1966 to undertake a year's research. He knew of Tiegerman's presence in the city, but in fact met him by chance at a restaurant. Tiegerman was taken aback to learn that Hungerford had also studied with Friedman. Tiegerman recalled a time when Friedman and his wife insisted that he join them in Leipzig in 1916 for Friedman's appearance with the Gewandhaus Orchestra under Nikisch. Friedman's wife had urged him to come backstage, as they had arranged for Tiegerman to be presented to Nikisch by her husband: shyness overcame him, however, and Tiegerman remained outside. He once confided to Hungerford that Friedman's pianism had declined in the late 1930s due to reduced practising and a desire to end decades of exhausting world tours.

Hungerford and Tiegerman felt an immediate empathy for one another. Tiegerman fêted his younger colleague after Hungerford's Cairo recitals. Numbering photography among his many talents, Hungerford took several portraits of Tiegerman. The 1967 Seven Day War abruptly ended part of Hungerford's work in Egypt. Although Jewish, Tiegerman never experienced animosity or restrictions after Egypt's Suez crisis and wars with Israel, which resulted in mass emigrations by entire communities of European origin. The following year he weakened and his health deteriorated rapidly after an inept prostate operation; he died in Cairo in 1968 at the age of 75. A niece from

Any worries Horowitz had would have subsided in 1931 when Tiegerman moved to Egypt, as his severe asthma demanded an arid climate. In Cairo, Tiegerman's infrequent recitals became events as significant as those by visitors such as Sauer, Cortot, Kempff and Bachauer. He lived alone, tranquilly, in Cairo until the end of his life, except for a year spent in Sudan to avoid a possible Nazi invasion of Egypt. A number of his concerto performances and studio recitals were frequently broadcast on Egyptian radio. A visit to their Babelian complex proved fruitless: according to one source, they had been erased, reused for newer versions by Barenboim and other contemporary pianists. Gone, too, are their archival tapes of the Cairo concerts given by Furtwängler and Clemens Krauss in the early 1950s. Future researchers must overcome impossible odds as the radio's highly-restricted, uncatalogued repository may contain tapes with proscribed political material.

Through the collaboration of Henri Barda, Selim Sednaoui (a pupil of Tiegerman and Michelangeli) and the Paris-based pianist Ramzi Yassa, a private recording of Tiegerman's 1963 farewell concert (Franck's *Symphonic Variations* and Saint-Saëns's Fifth Concerto) was traced,

Brno arrived after his death to settle his estate; perhaps she will be found and can help to locate his missing archive.

Prince Hassan, author, painter and sculptor, whose playing delighted Tiegerman and whose understanding of music is formidable, wrote that Tiegerman's passing left a void in the musical world and the lack of a monument to his accomplishments was tragic. He speculated why his teacher and friend chose to end his career with Saint-Saëns's *Egyptian* Concerto: Hassan believes it was Tiegerman's way of thanking Egypt for having sustained him and his health.

New listeners will hear the art of a once-lost master remembered only by those he played for and taught. Tiegerman's artistry represents a music-making which moved Friedman, intimidated Horowitz, and shaped the playing of Henri Barda and hundreds of pupils. The treasures retrieved in Egypt continue to surprise.**IPQ**

All photographs courtesy of Allan Evans

Review of 'Tiegerman: The Lost Legend of Cairo' on page 102

THE ART OF A LOST MASTER

Tiegerman: those he played for and those he taught

Ignace Tiegerman
Tiegerman: The Lost Legend of Cairo
(including a performance by Henri Barda, and the voice of Leschetizky)
Arbiter ℗ ARBITER116

Ignaz Friedman
Complete Solo Recordings
Pearl ℗ IF2000 (12/90)

Severin Eisenberger
Opal ℗ OPALCD9858 (1/96)

Henri Barda
Chopin Piano Sonatas
Calliope ℗ CAL9680
Liszt Piano Sonata etc
Calliope ℗ CAL6680
Ravel Chamber Music
Calliope ℗ CAL9822

Bruce Hungerford
The Legendary Hungerford
Vanguard Classics ℗ SVC76/9 (W/99)

WIN TOP-PRICE TICKETS

to *Marc-André Hamelin concerts* at the Wigmore Hall, London

We have two pairs of top-priced tickets to give to *IPQ* readers for each of Marc-André Hamelin's recitals on June 1st, 8th and 15th.

Tuesday, June 1st	
Alkan	Grande Sonate, 'Les Quatres Ages', Op. 33
Medtner	Sonata romantica in B flat minor, Op. 53 No 1
Eckhardt-Gramatté	Sonata No. 6 'Drei Klavierstücke'

Tuesday, June 8th	
Medtner	Sonata in E minor, 'Night wind', Op. 25
Schubert	Sonata in B flat, D960

Tuesday, June 15th	
Medtner	Sonate-idylle in G, Op. 56
Godowsky	Seven Studies after Chopin
Rzewski	The People United Will Never Be Defeated

To win a pair of tickets to one of these performances, answer the following question:
How many commercial solo recordings has Marc-André Hamelin released?

Send your answer on a postcard, by May 10th, to
IPQ Competition
135 Greenford Road
Sudbury Hill, Harrow
Middlesex, HA1 3YD

Please specify on your postcard which performances you would prefer to attend.

Winners will be notified by post and there is no cash alternative. The competition is open to all *IPQ* readers worldwide, but travel and accommodation is not included. Employees of Gramophone Publications, Georgina Ivor Associates and the Wigmore Hall may not enter. The Publisher's decision is final and no correspondence will be entered into. If you would prefer not to receive information about products and services we feel may be of interest, please let us know on your postcard.

Individuality with honour

ROB COWAN TALKS TO LEON FLEISHER ABOUT THE DANGERS OF EMULATING

PIANISTS OF THE PAST, BAD TASTE AND THE 'CHOLESTEROL'

THAT CLOGS MODERN MUSIC-MAKING

Energy and courage in the face of adversity are central to the character of pianist-conductor Leon Fleisher. Much has already been written of Fleisher's long-term battle with repetitive strain injury, his fight to recuperate, his resolve to hone a secure technique in others, and eventually, after much hard work, his valiant re-entry to the two-hand repertory.

His illness struck during the mid-1960s but now, with a wealth of educational experiences behind him (including an 11-year stint as Artistic Director of the Tanglewood Music Center), he is up and running as one of the major practising musicians of his generation. Countless works have been written especially for him, not least a Left-Hand Concerto by Lukas Foss, a Concerto for Three Hands (two hands at one piano, and one hand at another) by Gunther Schuller and an extraordinary Concerto by William Bolcom 'for two left hands and two pianos' for performance with Gary Graffman, who had suffered a condition similar to Fleisher's own.

Most know Fleisher as the masterful exponent of Beethoven and Brahms piano concertos in distinguished CBS/Sony recordings under George Szell. He is now playing the Brahms D minor again, though his overall tempo is slower than it once was. 'If I'm not mistaken, I used to play it in 44 minutes,' he reminisced last October; 'but somebody recently timed a version I did with Giulini who, I must say, was not in a hurry himself – and I think we

'The trouble is that a lot of young people think of freedom and individuality as finding a favourite note and sitting on it like a hen laying an egg.'

clocked in at 47 or 48 minutes.' And had the interpretative components of his performance changed? 'It's hard for me to say,' he replied. 'It's part of an ongoing process. The things that I knew before, I still know; but I'm constantly discovering new connections, new relationships, and new aspects of the score.'

Fleisher recalls, with some affection, his earliest successes – though he was amazed to note that a handful of them have since found their way on to 'unofficial' CDs. He remembered one occasion, ten or so years ago, when his wife was leafing through the racks in a record shop and suddenly chanced upon a certain pirate Mozart concerto recording. 'It was a performance of K488 that I played under Bruno Walter when I was 18 – my very first, as it happens. And it's not bad for a first K488, I must say. I remember being quite panic-stricken at the actual performance, but I listened to it again and was really rather impressed. I had a certain gift when I was 18. I've no idea what has happened to it since. I guess that stuff always comes back to bite you; there's probably more of it out there than I would care to think about.'

Recent CD successes have included the Korngold Suite for two violins, cello and piano left-hand (on Sony Classical), described by Fleisher as 'part-Mahler, part-Errol Flynn'. He claims never to have really enjoyed recording 'because, in a sense, I find it unsympathetic to an art which depends on renewal, spontaneity and the ability to grow and to change. Recording is of necessity a moment frozen in time, and after you get used to the gesture of a particular recorded performance, it's no longer fresh. There are other dangers, too. I would refer, for example, to one of the great pianists of the twentieth century, Vladimir Horowitz. He produced a very special sonority that was aided by the way he had his piano arranged. He preferred a very light action; his technician used lacquer and lacquer-thinners on the hammers to get a very brilliant sound. In fact, when you heard Horowitz live, the thing that

reproduce that kind of sound without realizing that there are many aspects and dimensions to it. But while Horowitz had his piano doped and Glenn Gould played only his own pianos, most young people have no choice of instrument.

Returning to the two-hand repertory: Leon Fleisher *Photo ICM Artists/Steiner*

most struck you about him – at least for the first minute or two – was that he sounded like a fire engine. But after a short while, his mastery of tonal variety and colour won through.'

Fleisher sees a real danger in the way some young players try to emulate old recordings. 'They tend to play on dead, dull pianos,' he says. 'They almost break their hands trying to

They don't realize that, especially in recording, these people had perfected the conditions that they demanded in order to help their specific sound.' He cites the dangers of playing with rounded, curved fingers – 'using the fingers as hammers' – as being especially dangerous. 'In trying to develop as much individual finger strength as possible, some youngsters forget that, comparatively speaking, the muscles where the fingers are connected to the hand are very prone to injury.' Fleisher notes how both Horowitz and Gould played with very long, straight fingers. 'Do you know of any teacher who talks of playing the piano with long, flat fingers?' he asks. 'Of course you don't!'

I have always thought of Fleisher the interpreter as poised between Apollonian and Dionysian viewpoints. The idea obviously amused him. 'I am sure these terms were invented by journalists,' he chuckled. 'People like to pigeon-hole other people; it gives them a sense of security. The idea that one has to be either Apollonian or Dionysian is so limiting. If you are an artist, you have an artistic kind of intelligence that informs your intuition, and your intuition responds by informing your intelligence. One creates a concept as a result of these two things, so how on earth can you separate them?'

One of Fleisher's earliest key influences was the great Austrian-born pianist and composer Artur Schnabel. And yet he claims that Schnabel has been widely misunderstood. 'Most people, in their lazy ways, describe him as intellectual. There was never, in my humble opinion, anybody as spontaneous, as inspired or as inspiring as Schnabel. His spontaneity took one to a totally different level of artistic awareness, but it was informed by his incredibly astute and perceptive vision of what a piece contained, of its form, its structure.'

Inevitably, one asks why there are no Schnabels, Fischers, Cortots, Friedmans or Horowitzes around today. Is the individuality that distinguished so many pianists of the past a sort of 'period' attribute? Fleisher thinks that, generally speaking, young people today have a fear of doing things in bad taste. 'That, plus the fact that when you are under stress, as at a public performance, the tendency is to contract – not only physically, but also emotionally and spiritually. When you make a pianistic leap at a concert and miss your target, you nearly always miss by undershooting – because your muscles are contracting, more so than in the practice studio. Also, the ability to be free really depends on how clearly you understand the form and structure of a piece, because freedom means – in a sense – bending the music. If you bend where there are musical 'joints', then there will always be a sense of inevitability and logic. The trouble is that a lot of young people think of freedom

and individuality as finding a favourite note and sitting on it like a hen laying an egg. As with bad tenors, that usually means a high note: they'll wait on it, or on a dissonance, or a suspension. But as they get older, they begin to learn more about music, learn to be freer "according to the music".'

And yet there are some freedoms that are musically inappropriate. Fleisher considers that the nineteenth century was a very dangerous period for the re-creation of music 'because performers began to emerge as a species apart from the composer-performer. They would usurp many responsibilities. If they felt like playing a *forte* where a composer marked *piano*, they would go ahead and do so – because 'they were the stars'. That was a terrible habit and music became unrecognizably distorted as a result of it. In my view there were two people in the twentieth century who restored musical interpretation to a proper balance: Schnabel and Toscanini. Both reinstated, in their different ways, an adherence to the Urtext and I think that we are still benefiting from their wisdom. The next generation – and by that I mean the likes of Barenboim, Brendel, Perahia, Schiff and Lupu – all based their approach on the Schnabelian precept that the text is the proper point of departure. That's where we start – and one's own intuitiveness, one's own intelligence, brings out the individualities from that point of view.'

'Individuality with honour', perhaps. But what about the fashionable drive towards 'authentic' performance practice? 'Generally speaking, there's much too much cholesterol in modern music-making anyway. Or, to carry a metaphor to its death, it clogs the musical arteries. But the reversion back to original instruments was already being done back in the 1920s. It's nothing new.' Fleisher blames Wagner for some of the century's worst interpretative excesses. 'Even the sainted Klemperer and Karajan carried through this bloated approach to Beethoven, even Mozart. That's all due to Mr Wagner. He had a terrible influence. There is a very common problem with the performance of music of the classical era – and by that I mean everyone before, let's say, Schumann. Many people use what you might call romantic devices in playing classical repertoire, and it doesn't work. Horowitz's recordings of Schubert's B flat Piano Sonata,

D960 are, in my view, unsuccessful primarily because they are filled with romantic devices applied to Schubert.' But is it possible to employ successfully classical devices for the interpretation of romantic music? 'Yes, because historically it's correct. That's why Roger [Norrington] and [Frans] Brüggen and all these people who have specialized in baroque and classical repertory are now advancing into later music. That works better, because it reflects a historical process, a continuation. But to take romantic or contemporary devices and apply them to older works is, I think, ridiculous. It makes them sound like nonsense.'

Romanticizing music from the classical eras and earlier is one thing, but I do sometimes wonder whether the political and cultural traumas that have raped our century – certainly over the last 60 or so years – have inhibited our approach to romantic music. We don't seem to believe in it in the way that we once did. Fleisher ponders the point. 'There are two possible reasons for that,' he says. 'Firstly, our lives, for whatever reason, have increasingly become so vulgarized, manipulated and commercialized that it's very difficult to return to the heroic

world of Liszt with the requisite innocence. Everything has been "soap-opera-ized" since then. It's spoiled for us. Second, there is so much happening today that is unbearable that young people in particular build protective walls around themselves. You walk down the street and you see homeless people in winter time; you see hungry people; you see things going on all over the world that are absolutely insupportable in human terms. If we were to react to them, we would perpetually be in tears. We then come to music, but we still have these defences intact when we should be absolutely defenceless against the change of one note in the harmony that turns cloud into sunshine. For any musician, even the smallest detail has to be meaningful.

'So, you tell me, how is it possible to switch from being defended in everyday life to suddenly dropping all those defences when you become involved with art? What you hear, therefore, is emotionally and spiritually blocked, performances that concentrate almost exclusively on a kind of physical mastery that's very boring – which is why nowadays so many players sound alike.' **IPQ**

LEON FLEISHER: THE COMPLETE DISCOGRAPHY

Compiled by Donald Manildi

Composer	Work	Record company & number	Date
Bach	Chaconne (arr. Brahms)[1]	Sony Classical ① SK48081	1992
	Jesu, Joy of Man's Desiring (arr. Hess)	Sony Classical ① MLK45627	c1963
Beethoven	Piano Concertos Nos.1-5	Sony Classical ① SB3K48397	1959 (No. 4); 1961
	(Cleveland Orch / Szell)		
	Piano Concerto No. 4	Enterprise ① 4189; Hunt ① 733	1956*
	(Cologne Radio Orch / Klemperer)		
Blumenfeld	Etude for the Left Hand, Op. 36[1]	Sony Classical ① SK48081	1992
Brahms	Piano Concertos Nos. 1 & 2	Sony Classical ① MH2K63225	1958 (No. 1); 1962
	(Cleveland Orch / Szell)		
	Piano Quintet, Op. 34	Odyssey ⊙ Y35211	1963
	(Juilliard Qt)		
	Liebeslieder Waltzes, Op. 52	Sony Classical ① SBK48176	1960
	(R. Serkin, Valente, Kleinman, Conner, Singher)		
	Handel Variations, Op. 24	Sony Classical ① MH2K63225	1956
	Waltzes, Op. 39	Sony Classical ① MH2K63225	1956
Britten	Diversions for Piano and Orchestra[1]	Desto ⊙ DC7168	1974
	(Baltimore SO / Comissiona)		
	(Boston SO / Ozawa)	Sony Classical ① SK47188	1990
Copland	Piano Sonata	Philips ① 456 775-2PM2	1963
Debussy	Suite bergamasque	Epic ⊙ LC3554	1958
Franck	Symphonic Variations	Sony Classical ① MYK37812	1956
	(Cleveland Orch / Szell)		
Grieg	Piano Concerto, Op. 16	Sony Classical ① MPK44849	1960
	(Cleveland Orch / Szell)		
Hindemith	The Four Temperaments	Epic ⊙ LC3356	1956
	(Netherlands Ch Orch / Goldberg)		
Kirchner	Piano Sonata	Epic ⊙ BC1262	1963
Korngold	Suite for Piano and Strings, Op. 23[1]	Sony Classical ① SK48253	1991
	(Silverstein, Smirnoff, Ma)		
Liszt	Piano Sonata in B minor	Philips ① 456 775-2PM2	1959
Mozart	Piano Concerto No. 23, K488	AS Disc ① 412	1949*
	(Los Angeles PO / Walter)		
	Piano Concerto No. 25, K503	Sony Classical ① MYK37762	1959
	(Cleveland Orch / Szell)		
	Rondo in D, K485	Epic ⊙ LC3584	1958
	Piano Sonata No. 4, K282	Epic ⊙ LC3584	1958

Mozart	Piano Sonata No. 10, K330	Philips ① 456 775-2PM2	1958
Prokofiev	Piano Concerto No. 4, Op. 53[1] (Boston SO / Ozawa)	Sony Classical ① SK47188	1991
Rachmaninov	Rhapsody on a Theme of Paganini (Cleveland Orch / Szell)	Philips ① 456 775-2PM2 Sony Classical ① MYK37812	1956
Ravel	Piano Concerto in D for the Left Hand[1] (Baltimore SO / Comissiona)	Philips ① 456 775-2PM2	1982
	(Boston SO / Ozawa)	Sony Classical ① SK47188	1990
	Miroirs – Alborada del gracioso	Philips ① 456 775-2PM2	1958
	Sonatine	Philips ① 456 775-2PM2	1958
	Valses nobles et sentimentales	Epic ⊙ LC3554	1958
Rorem	Three Barcarolles	Philips ① 456 775-2PM2	1963
Saint-Saëns	Six Etudes, Op. 135[1]	Sony Classical ① SK48081	1992
Saxton	Chacony[1]	Sony Classical ① SK48081	1992
Schmidt	Piano Quintet[1] (1926) (Silverstein, Smirnoff, Tree, Ma)	Sony Classical ① SK48253	1993
Schubert	Wanderer Fantasy, D760	Sony Classical ① SBK47667	1963
	Ländler, D790, Nos. 1-8	Columbia ⊙ ML5061	1954
	Piano Sonata in A, D664	Sony Classical ① SBK47667	1963
	Piano Sonata in B flat, D960	Columbia ⊙ ML5061	1954
Schumann	Piano Concerto, Op. 54 (Cleveland Orch / Szell)	Sony Classical ① MPK44849	1960
	Dichterliebe, Op. 48 (Shirley-Quirk)	Arabesque ① Z6700	1996
	Liederkreis, Op. 24 (Shirley-Quirk)	Arabesque ① Z6700	1996
	Frauenliebe und -leben, Op. 42 (Bryn-Julson)	Arabesque ① Z6700	1996
Scriabin	Prélude and Nocturne, Op. 9[1]	Sony Classical ① SK48081	1992
Sessions	From My Diary	Epic ⊙ BC1262	1963
J. Strauss II	Gypsy Baron Waltzes[1] (arr. Godowsky)	Sony Classical ① SK48081	1992
Takács	Toccata and Fugue, Op. 56[1]	Sony Classical ① SK48081	1992
Weber	Invitation to the Dance, Op. 65	Epic ⊙ LC3675	1959
	Piano Sonata No. 4, Op. 70	Philips ① 456 775-2PM2	1959

Notes

Dates followed by * indicate live recording

Items marked [1] are for left hand only

Catalogue numbers are given only for current, or most recently available, editions

A star in the making

Harriet Smith reviews Volodos's latest offering: his Carnegie Hall début

The first thing that strikes you about Volodos's second recital disc (a follow-up to his highly praised recording of piano transcriptions, ① SK62691, A/97), is the apparent imbalance of the programme: lots of very short tracks, the only one of any significant length being Scriabin's Tenth Sonata. Examining the track-listing more closely, you notice that even though the featured composers are all mainstream romantics, Volodos shows a pronounced preference for some of their more obscure offerings.

On playing the disc, two sensations recalled from the earlier recording are immediately recollected and reinforced: the unobtrusiveness of Volodos's virtuosity and his remarkable ability to spin and sing a melodic line. Jagged edges are not in his repertoire. I can't think of another pianist performing today who makes the instrument *sound* so consistently seductive. In his version of the Liszt/Horowitz 15th *Hungarian Rhapsody* (which deviates from Horowitz's version only in very minor respects) extreme technical demands cease to be an issue – he performs the work imperiously but does not subscribe to the 'see what I can do' school of virtuosity. His *crescendos* engulf with all the force of a tidal wave but the piano never becomes harsh. Comparison with Horowitz's own performance (RCA ① GD87755, 9/90) is instructive as they are remarkably similar in conception, only the rougher recording making the older pianist sometimes appear a degree less clear-cut.

If the Liszt – which offers an obvious opportunity to dazzle – in Volodos's hands possesses an understated kind of glamour, how much more pronounced is this in the more introspective pieces. His Rachmaninov selection is perhaps the highlight of an outstanding disc. To some, who have grown up admiring Ashkenazy's *Etudes-tableaux* (Decca ⊙ SXL6604, 5/73, and London

① 566 234-2LC6, 6/88ᴿ), Volodos's reading of the D minor might seem too understated. To my ears, however, both this and the C minor are enormously effective, the pianist conveying all the intimacy and subtlety of the music. Crude point-making (which for too many pianists seems to be an essential part of Rachmaninov 'interpretation') is entirely absent. Though Volodos is very quick to react to mood changes – the *tempo più vivo* in Op. 39 No. 8 is suitably skittish, and all is so imaginatively coloured that it seems as if an orchestra were at work – it's all perfectly scaled, with none of that all-too-common surging towards tops of phrases. In Op. 33 No. 3 Volodos delights in rich sonorities and painstaking (though entirely natural-sounding) dynamic gradations, and he has the advantage of a left-hand big enough to cope with the chordal writing without arpeggiation. The *Meno mosso* is yet another instance of a beautifully sung line, but touch and rhythmic subtlety also play their part in forming such perfectly breathed lines.

Similarly, the A flat *Fragment* is not only impeccably voiced and shaped, but also imbued with an unforced sadness (could any non-Russian pianist make it sound quite this poignant?) that is very compelling. By comparison, in Howard Shelley's hands (Hyperion ① CDA66198, 9/87) the piece appears prosaic, though, interestingly, his chosen tempos are similar.

It is only in the Scriabin group that doubts arise: a suspicion, particularly in the Tenth Sonata, that Volodos is underplaying the interpretative possibilities of this music. Like everything else here, there's no question that it's beautifully performed. Op. 52 No. 2 again has that breathtaking lightness which never fails to thrill. But reactions to markings such as *voluptueux* are too understated. Horowitz (Sony Classical ① CD42411, 4/90) is more characterful, even if he is inclined to play fast and loose with some of the rhythms. Where Volodos is reasoned, Horowitz is histrionic, and ultimately that's what this music needs to thrive.

Schumann's *Bunte Blätter*, on the other hand, receives a very fine performance, proving an ideal vehicle for Volodos's effortless brand of lyricism. The very first note, perfectly sung, promises much, and what follows more than lives up to that expectation. One of his greatest gifts is to take the simplest piece and nourish it with a fantastic range of colour and phrasing. Try No. 6, or No. 8, and revel in the way his attention to detail in turn creates an overall shape, how the ravishing colour palette elevates each of these pieces to perfectly formed gems. Even in No. 7, where someone can be heard getting up from his seat and leaving the hall, Volodos's attention doesn't waver for a second. No. 11, one of the masterpieces in the set, is here taken at a very measured tempo (lasting 8'58"), yet the phrasing is such that it never becomes portentous. And in the last piece, finding Schumann at his most high-spirited, there's no lack of ebullience or tender good humour. Where the Schumann of his fellow Russian and contemporary, Evgeni Kissin, is all vehemence and ruthless virtuosity, Arcadi Volodos is altogether gentler, and sounds more in sympathy with the composer.

In his first disc Volodos brought the house down with his wickedly amusing (or, to some ears, merely outrageous) transcription of Mozart's *Turkish Rondo*. This time it's the turn of the Mendelssohn/Liszt/Horowitz *Wedding March*, which he treats to one further transformation, in the process adding his name to those of his illustrious forebears. Volodos takes Horowitz's version (which he recorded only once – RCA ℗ GD87755, 9/90) as his starting-point, but shortens it by removing most of the more *espressivo* portions, turning it into more of a showpiece,

with fewer lyrical detours. Again one experiences the spine-tingling juxtaposition of the most *leggierissimo*, *prestissimo* passagework set against thundering sonorities as Volodos races up and down the keyboard with all the power of Thor. It's a *tour de force*, in places even out-Horowitzing Horowitz. Comparison with former Horowitz-pupil, Ivan Davis (Decca ⊙ SXL6415), is also instructive. He sticks closely to Liszt's version, only throwing in the occasional Horowitzism, and while he demonstrates a brilliant, glinting virtuosity, Davis lacks the extremes of dynamics which make the Volodos performance so thrilling.

The running order discomfits in only one respect, though it has been changed from the original order which crept in with the Scriabin triumvirate (almost inaudible in the concert since the audience was still piling through the doors). Positioning the Scriabin *Prélude*, Op. 2 No. 2 after the *Wedding March* (complete with delighted response from the – now fully engaged – audience) was presumably done to suggest the idea of an encore (of which, in the actual concert these were but two out of a total of six). But the applause makes you feel as if you've come to the end of the disc and then the final track appears almost as if by accident. To my mind the disc should ideally have ended with the *Wedding March*, leaving the listener to pick his jaw up off the floor before pressing the play button again!

The recording – which contrary to the claim on the jewel-case doesn't sound entirely live – has an appealing rounded warmth to it, effectively capturing the sound as remembered from the hall itself. Harris Goldsmith's notes provide a perceptive mini-review of the event. Let's hope that Volodos follows up this disc with the rumoured Rachmaninov Second and Third Concertos – and that we don't have to wait another 18 months for his next release. **IPQ**

RECORDING DETAILS

Arcadi Volodos at Carnegie Hall
Arcadi Volodos (pf).
Sony Classical ℗ ⊙ SM60893;
ⓒ SK60893 (72 minutes: DDD).
Recorded at a performance in
Carnegie Hall, New York on
October 21st, 1998.
Liszt (arr. Horowitz): Hungarian
Rhapsody No. 15 in A minor,
'Rákóczy March', S244.
Mendelssohn/Liszt (arr. Horowitz):
A Midsummer Night's Dream –
Wedding March, S410.
Rachmaninov: Fragment in A flat.
Etudes-tableaux – D minor, Op. 39
No. 8; C minor, Op. 33 No. 3.
Schumann: Bunte Blätter, Op. 99.
Scriabin: Piano Sonata No. 10 in C,
Op. 70. Enigma, Op. 52 No. 2.
Caresse dansée, Op. 57 No. 2.
Prelude in B, Op. 2 No. 2.

CD Reviews

Bach French Suite No. 5 in G, BWV816. Overture in the French style in B minor, BWV831. **Piotr Anderszewski** (pf). Harmonia Mundi Les Nouveaux Interprètes ® ① HMN91 1679 (53 minutes: DDD).

Having previously appeared on two Philips discs as Viktoria Mullova's partner in the three violin sonatas of Brahms (① 446 709-2PH, 5/97) plus a mix of Debussy, Janáček and Prokofiev sonatas (① 446 091-2PH, 1/96), as well as a Polish PolyGram collection of solo works by Bach, Beethoven and Webern (which received a Polish record prize in 1996 – ① 011 306-2), the 29-year-old Piotr Anderszewski can now be heard in an all-Bach programme on Harmonia Mundi'. His studies have taken him to a widely-distanced series of institutions: the conservatories at Lyon and Strasbourg, the University of Southern California and the Chopin Academy in Warsaw. His international appearances have an even greater compass, and he has been heard throughout Europe, especially Britain, and the United States. His musical interests, to judge from his choice of repertoire, often involve works with formidable structural and intellectual features, and it is clear that he is a most

serious young musician. Of the two works on this disc, the lengthy *French Overture* was, I have reliably been informed, actually chosen by him as an encore following a recital in London's Wigmore Hall last year. One is reminded of the tale of Rudolf Serkin's Berlin début, when he reportedly played the *Goldberg Variations* as an encore.

Judging from his rendition of the *Overture* plus the somewhat more lightweight Fifth *French Suite* which precedes it, Anderszewski appears to be an interesting amalgam of Bach *à la* Schiff, Gould and Richter (but with sparing use of pedal). The kind of pianist who obviously savours intellectual exercise, the performer begins the Allemande of his *French Suite* with highly detailed articulation and a presumed sense of baroque style as transferred to the piano. He even adds ornaments and a few melodic decoration on repeats, although trills tend to be inexpressively fast. The sprightly, rhythmically tight Courante, however, begins to show certain mannerisms, such as hints of the overblown dynamics that so often are to permeate his *French Overture*. By the time one gets to his contrasted, rather hushed Sarabande, rhythmically too loose to conform to the dance (its opposing number in the *Overture* is even more precious), one begins to recognize that this is an intellect playing with Bach, just as so often occurs in Gould's recordings.

Curiously, an inappropriate lack of articulation occurs in the *French Suite*'s overly *legato* Gigue, which is why there seem to be so many styles to his essentially post-romantic but emotionally impersonal interpretations. In no respect can one argue against the pianist's understanding of Bach's contrapuntal lines, but the effect of his technically skilled playing seems to me almost facile, even a touch glib, a reaction that occurred more emphatically upon a second hearing of the disc, when Anderszewski's dynamic and rhythmic idiosyncrasies began to outweigh the subject. It is possible that some listeners will find his way with Bach intriguing, but personally I would opt for András Schiff (Decca ⓓ 452 279-2DM12, 3/97). **Igor Kipnis**

....

Bach Six Partitas, BWV825-30 – No. 1 in B flat; No. 4 in D. Solo Violin Sonata No. 1 in G minor, BWV1001 (arr. Fiorentino). **Sergio Fiorentino** (pf). APR ⓔ ⓓ APR5558 (76 minutes: DDD).

Sergio Fiorentino's recent death was a great loss to the music world. Although he never received the acclaim and recognition he deserved during his lifetime, he left a startlingly large LP discography that centred on Chopin, Liszt, Rachmaninov and Schumann, as well as many transcriptions. Fiorentino's repertoire was far more comprehensive than this implies, however, and APR's Fiorentino Edition is helping to fill in some of the gaps. Previous issues added Scriabin, Schubert and Prokofiev to his recorded legacy, and now we have Bach *Partitas*.

Fiorentino's Bach will not be to all tastes and is bound to raise some eyebrows; his tempos are often on the slow side, and his choice of articulation can be unusual. What some will find more unsettling is his willingness to expand upon Bach's harmonies (always tastefully) and his practice of horizontally filling in Bach's bass-lines in slow movements.

Fiorentino's approach works particularly well in the First *Partita* where, rather than boldly forcing his ideas upon the listener, his deeply personal and introspective playing draws the listener into his world. There is a wonderful

sense of clarity in his playing and great attention is paid to direction of line; moreover, the heightened sensitivity shows how dear this music was to him. Fiorentino's handling of the Fourth *Partita* is even more individual, but perhaps less convincing. The Allemande, for example, is taken at an extraordinarily slow tempo which, while initially intriguing, results in the movement lasting over 15 minutes. All repeats are taken throughout the disc, and in this Allemande movement, the bass-line is thoroughly embellished during repeats.

Although Fiorentino played and recorded many Bach transcriptions, this one of the G minor Violin Sonata is new to his discography. Those familiar with Godowsky's arrangement of this sonata will find that the two have little in common. Fiorentino's transcription eschews nineteenth- and twentieth-century devices, instead attempting to emulate what the master himself might have written had he decided to make a keyboard arrangement of this work. Fiorentino's performance contains some of the most captivating playing on the disc, with truly masterful phrasing.

Remarkably, for all of Fiorentino's individuality, one never senses anything contrived about the performances. At his best, Fiorentino could play as well as any of this century's great pianists, and although APR's series certainly has its ups and downs, the moments of inspiration make the discs well worth investigating. **Farhan Malik**

....

Bach Six English Suites, BWV806-11 – No. 2 in A minor; No. 4 in F; No. 5 in E minor. **Murray Perahia** (pf). Sony Classical ⓔ ⓓ SK60277 (62 minutes: DDD).

Of Murray Perahia's first set of Bach *English Suites* David Fanning's concluding judgement (Su/98) was 'This is a CD to treasure'. The second set is no less so. This Sony disc, at once attractively spacious and intelligently focused in its representation of instrumental tone, provides enthralling linked examples of both the pianist's art and the art of Bach playing.

Indeed, it is the maturity of the former that affords so many revelations of the latter. Perahia's command of these works is masterly – not just of the notes, which in the case of this pianist (though not many others alive) perhaps goes without saying, but also of the larger patterns and purposes beneath these notes. In both the local and the global sense his playing is wonderfully shapely. Every phrase possesses its own carefully chosen characterization in terms of colour, weight, lyrical address, rhythmic definition, foreground-and-background balance and dramatic directionality; at the same time the feeling of 'connectedness', of phrases unerringly thought through and built up into whole movements, imbues these performances with a peculiar vigour and radiance. Intellectually, physically – because few modern Bach records add up to so strong a statement of faith in the aptness of the modern piano for this composer's music, all the stronger for being entirely free of show, fuss or self-regard – and spiritually, the match here of music and interpreter is endlessly satisfying.

Given all this, to single out for special praise one of the performances, when all three have so much to offer, probably says more about the reviewer's personal taste than about the pianist's achievement; but I found the reading of the F major the pick of the three in its combination of an almost pastoral grace in the singing line, charm, captivating wit (Perahia's recent embrace of Scarlatti sonatas is obviously pertinent here – Sony Classical ① SK62785, 5/97), rhythmic buoyancy and an acutely judged prayerful hush in the Sarabande. The account of the A minor, so beautifully contained and limpid in its tones and interweavings of voice, approaches the music in a manner entirely different from that of Argerich in her dazzling 1979 DG recording (① 453 572-2GAC3, A/97): her tingling vitality, lack of emotional inhibition and unbridled enthusiasm for the 'animal' excitement of linear interplay make for a Bach keyboard experience of unequalled exhilaration. Maybe it was because of a lingering Argerich post-echo that Perahia's traversal of the A minor Allemande sounded to me faintly artificial in its *Affekt* – the pathos seems laid on, not with a trowel exactly, but with a super-refinement of touch and dynamic variation that came to feel, in context, ever so slightly calculated.

Against this one sets innumerable examples of sheer felicity elsewhere in Perahia's playing. Let me give just two: the expressive resourcefulness of the F major Allemande, with its delicious savouring of triplet figuration, and the culminating power and force of the E minor Gigue, which balances contrapuntal complexity and athletic boldness. The continual enrichment of Perahia's repertory and deepening of his artistry offer bounteous present satisfactions and, even more important, promise infinite rewards for the future.   **Max Loppert**

....

Bach Six Partitas, BWV825-30 – No. 2 in C minor; No. 4 in D; No. 5 in G. **Richard Goode** (pf). Nonesuch ℗ ① 7559-79483-2 (72 minutes: DDD).

Bach, as Busoni once claimed, may be the foundation of piano playing, but are his keyboard works best suited to the instruments of the composer's time? Landowska thought so, and her influence has largely prevailed in an era dominated by period performances. That hasn't prevented pianists like Rosalyn Tureck, Glenn Gould, András Schiff and Angela Hewitt from specializing in Bach on the modern concert grand. Then there are pianists who suddenly focus on Bach at the mid-point of their careers. These include such eminences as Alfred Brendel, Daniel Barenboim, Murray Perahia and now Richard Goode, with the first instalment of a cycle devoted to the Six *Partitas*.

One need not specialize to have a pronounced affinity for a composer, and Goode's fluid, unpressured way with these works mirrors the ease and naturalness with which his one-time mentor Mieczyslaw Horszowski navigated Bach's contrapuntal thickets. If Hewitt's nuanced, upholstered pianism (Hyperion ① CDA67191/2, 6/97) conjures up images of a chamber orchestra, Goode shapes the music like a singer whose breathing is noticeable but unobtrusive, as he follows Bach's melodic discourse over the bar-lines. Vocalism also informs Goode's tempo choices, which never fall outside the range of singability. Try humming along, for instance, with the gnarly gigues concluding the D major and G major *Partitas* (Nos. 4 and 5), and be surprised how many notes you get in!

Some listeners, to be sure, will miss the individual profile, hair-trigger rhythm and theatricality Gould brings to this music, particularly his CBC disc of No. 5 (① PSCD2005) and the blazing video version of No. 4 featured in 'The Question of Instrument' (The Glenn

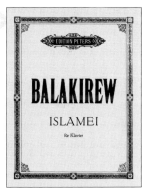

Gould Collection, Vol. 14 – Sony Classical [CD] SHV48425). And even the Canadian cannot begin to approach Tureck's microscopic gradations of touch, studied though they may be (recently reissued in Philips's Great Pianists series – ① 456 976-2PM2). András Schiff's *Partitas* stand out for the pianist's warm, beefy sonority and ornamental audacity, a trait that may not be to all tastes. Yet Goode has clearly lived with and thought about these extraordinary, variegated works. The performances may not immediately grab your attention, but they grow on you with each listening. What's more, the pianist achieves a communicative ease that has previously often eluded him in the studio. Max Wilcox's production conveys presence and transparency that perfectly suit both music and pianist. I eagerly await the next volume.

Jed Distler

....

Beethoven Concerto for Piano and Orchestra No. 4 in G, Op. 58[a].
Schumann Concerto for Piano and Orchestra in A minor, Op. 54[b]. **Noel Mewton-Wood** (pf); [a]**Utrecht Symphony Orchestra,** [b]**Netherlands Philharmonic Orchestra /** [ab]**Walter Goehr.**
Dante Historical Piano Collection mono Ⓟ ① HPC106 (65 minutes: ADD). Item marked [a] from Musical Masterpiece Society MMS24, [b]MMS43 (both recorded *c*1952).

Noel Mewton-Wood's story – his marvellous early promise and then his extraordinary career, so rich in promise, so tragically truncated by his suicide at the age of 31 – was told by Cyrus Meher-Homji in the Winter 1999 issue of *IPQ*. Among the all-too-few records Mewton-Wood made between 1941 and 1953 were 11 of concerto or *concertante* works – notably the two by Chopin (Vol. 1 of Dante's series, W/99), all three by Tchaikovsky plus his *Concert Fantasia*, the Bliss, the Stravinsky piano-and-wind, the First Shostakovich and the raptly beautiful, poetic and finely-drawn accounts of Beethoven's Fourth and Schumann which form Dante's Vol. 2.

I have not heard the Chopin concertos; indeed, prior to these Beethoven and Schumann encounters I knew Mewton-Wood only from the famous and magnificent version of Tippett's song-cycle *Boyhood's End* that he – replacing Britten, the 'creator'-pianist – and Peter Pears recorded in 1952 (Argo ☉ RG15), itself long overdue for CD reissue. On the evidence of Vol. 2 alone, Mewton-Wood's reputation deserves the widest reappraisal: for he was plainly an artist of very special stamp and a technician of very high calibre.

What I admire most in both performances is their unfailing combination of qualities rarely matched, let alone so distinctively combined: punctilious attack, imaginative spontaneity, real authority and originality of musical viewpoint, genuine vigour and forcefulness of statement, an underlying emotional intensity, and the most exquisite refinement – never faked or 'put on' – in the control of tone colour and shading of dynamics. As Meher-Homji reported, one flaw in Mewton-Wood's live performances could be an occasional 'going through the tone' in loud passages; there is no hint of that here. In his excellent booklet-note, Jean-Charles Hoffelé, co-producer of the Dante disc, essays comparisons with Solomon – whose 'jeu intense et subtil' Mewton-Wood's elegant art, according to Hoffelé, recalls – and the young Perahia. I would also want to bring Curzon into the discussion: both he and Mewton-Wood studied with Schnabel, and the extreme delicacies and refinements that informed the palettes of both never at any time led to a wilting or anaemic musical outlook.

Mewton-Wood was, on this evidence, a pianist's pianist; even more important, he played – Neville Cardus noted, and he was not alone in doing so – like a composer (which he was), or, as Cardus put it, in a way that '[absorbed] himself in the composer's mind, not merely the composer's notes.' His rhythms possess a sharp definition and sense of purpose (it's no surprise that he was regarded as an inspired interpreter of both Stravinsky and Tippett); in the closing bars of the Schumann first movement, his impulsiveness in articulating triplet figuration brings with it a surge and conclusiveness that draw one's ears to the music in fresh and unexpected ways. One wants to borrow terms such as *vagando* to describe the manner in which, in the 'Intermezzo', the pianist wanders in his fantasy, pausing to admire the viewpoint (without ever risking, it should be noted, extravagant deformations of tempo), and formulating pianistic responses of the purest, most intimate poetry.

Gramophone's quarterly magazines for the collector

International Classical Record Collector

Edited by Tully Potter

International Classical Record Collector is the magazine for the collector of classical music recordings on all formats, from cylinders and 78s to analogue LPs and historic reissues on CD.

The Spring issue of *ICRC* pays tribute to a trio of artists: Florence Austral, a famous Brünnhilde of her day, whom Fred Gaisberg described as 'the most important recording soprano' of the early 1920s; her frequent 'partner in crime' was the tenor Walter Widdop, still the only tenor to have sung all the major Wagnerian roles; and the third is the conductor Albert Coates, a conductor who very clearly lost out when it came to leaving an adequate recorded legacy.

ICRC is published in Spring (February), Summer (May), Autumn (August) and Winter (November).

International Opera Collector

Edited by Michael Oliver

International Opera Collector is the only publication for the collector of opera recordings, past and present, that deals comprehensively with recorded opera on all formats.

In the Spring issue of *IOC*, Hugh Canning reveals his favourite Marschallins on disc. Bayreuth queen Astrid Varnay looks back over her career and recalls the legendary 1951 recording of Götterdämmerung, Gerard McBurney finds out what Mark-Anthony Turnage is up to, and Michael Oliver is in conversation with Antonio Pappano.

IOC is published in Spring (March), Summer (June), Autumn (September) and Winter (December).

To subscribe to *IOC* or *ICRC*, please telephone our credit card hotline on +44 (0)181-422 4562 and ask for *IOC* or *ICRC* Subscriptions.

Single copies are also available from specialist record stores.

Gramophone Publications Ltd, 135 Greenford Rd, Sudbury Hill, Harrow, Middlesex HA1 3YD, Great Britain
Fax +44 (0)181-869 8400   **E-mail** info@gramophone.co.uk

The taste – always a dangerous word to use, but necessary and appropriate here – of this Schumann reading is quite wonderfully sure; by its light even so highly praised a modern reading as Perahia's (with Sir Colin Davis as conductor – Sony Classical ① SK44899, 5/89) seems curiously rigid and monochrome. So, too, the Beethoven, whose start – the emergence of the solo voice out of silence – elicits playing of uncommon containment as well as uncommon beauty, with not a hint of indulgence in the phrasing and with an inborn (and in-turned) sense of dramatic argument; the marriage of forcefulness and gentleness dominates throughout. Both concerto performances are wholes: in spite of the sour wind and thin strings that characterize both Dutch orchestras, and in spite, of course, of the limited recording range, I've come to admire very much Goehr's sentient accompaniments. They 'place' with unfailing acuity the characteristics of the pianist and, in the Beethoven *Andante*, provide exactly the right dramatic contrast – brusque, sharp-edged tutti – to the exquisite pathos that Mewton-Wood finds in the solo writing.

Since receiving the CD for review I've returned to it many times, and gone for excited comparison to numerous versions of both works old and new in my library. On each occasion the result has been to discover that Mewton-Wood demands ranking on the highest levels of interpretation. **Max Loppert**

....

Beethoven Piano Sonatas – No. 8 in C minor, 'Pathétique', Op. 13[a]; No. 23 in F minor, 'Appassionata', Op. 57[b]. Piano Trio No. 7 in B flat, 'Archduke', Op. 97[c]. **William Murdoch** (pf). [c]**Albert Sammons** (vn); [c]**William H. Squire** (vc).
Pearl mono Ⓜ ① GEM0044 (67 minutes: ADD). Item marked [a] from Columbia L1849/50 (4/27), [b]L1906/8 (4/27), [c]L1851/5 (4/27).

William Murdoch was born in Australia in 1888, moving to London in 1906 when he won a scholarship to the Royal College of Music. He pursued a career as a pianist and chamber musician and taught at the Royal Academy of Music from 1930-6; he died in 1942. Murdoch made many records of short encores for Columbia and Decca – Chopin *Waltzes*, Debussy *Préludes*,

pieces by Grieg, Mendelssohn, Schutt, de Falla, Albéniz and such bravura works as Liszt's *La campanella* and 12th *Hungarian Rhapsody*.

What we have here is Murdoch's début on CD in three works of Beethoven recorded for the centenary year of 1927. Frederic Lamond recorded the *Pathétique* Sonata a few days after Murdoch for the rival HMV company (Biddulph ① LHW042, Sp/98) and it is fascinating to compare the beginning of this sonata because the performances are so different. Lamond is dramatic and commanding, with a fair amount of rubato while Murdoch is less flexible, with much tighter rhythms. Overall, Murdoch takes the outer movements quickly and the *Allegro molto e con brio* is just that, and perfectly controlled. I could hardly believe that the timings of the first movement were identical – Murdoch gives the feeling of a much faster performance but the playing is always fleet and clear. However, the Rondo does seem a little too fast, especially at the appearance of the triplets. The *Appassionata* gets similar treatment although the *ma non troppo* is closely observed in the third movement, creating a greater contrast with the extreme tempo of the concluding *Presto*. Although these performances are enjoyable I did feel that there was something lacking in terms of depth and insight; Murdoch plays fast but does not necessarily generate excitement, giving less of a sense of struggle in this dramatic music. The *Archduke* Trio, however, is a delight, with playing of the utmost geniality and unity.

In the booklet-notes Donald Manildi has managed to find a good deal of information on this rather elusive artist and although no recording details are given in the booklet (apart from the year of recording), they were made in the Wigmore Hall on October 12th, 1926 (*Pathétique*), November 18th, 1926 (*Archduke*) and January 19th and 20th, 1927 (*Appassionata*). The transfers, by Seth Winner, are very good indeed, especially in the Trio, with little surface noise and lifelike piano and string tone. *The Gramophone* of 1927 stated: 'one notices that the cello has a rather nasal quality, and that the piano, when accompanying, is almost inaudible.' This is not the case at all with this transfer. The microphone is placed rather far back in the hall for the sonatas, but the sound is still clear.

Anyone curious to hear Murdoch should not hesitate to obtain this CD and I hope more of his recordings will appear in the future to give us a fuller picture of his talents.

Jonathan Summers

Brahms Concerto for Piano and Orchestra No. 1 in D minor, Op. 15[a].
Mozart Concerto for Piano and Orchestra No. 23 in A, K488[b]. **Sir Clifford Curzon** (pf); **National Symphony Orchestra / [a]Enrique Jordá, [b]Boyd Neel.**
Dutton Laboratories Essential Archive mono ℗ ① CDEA5507 (72 minutes: ADD). Item marked [a] from Decca K1491/6 (10/47), [b]K1394/6 (6/48).

It is heartening to see companies mining the riches of Clifford Curzon's 78rpm legacy, bringing out many items that appear for the first time in a long-playing format. This disc contains the first versions of the only two works that Curzon recorded and approved for commercial issue three times. The annotations include snippets of reviews from the *EMG Monthly Newsletter* dating from when these 1945 (Mozart) and 1946 (Brahms) performances were first issued, and the comments largely hold true. In the Mozart, for example, *EMG*'s reviewer cited the lack of richness in the piano's lower register, and a kind of classical understatement from the pianist that only lightly touches on the slow movement's tragic character. Curzon is best in the rollicking finale, pointing up the music's wit with rippling passagework and economic accentuation. While one misses the added nuances and shadings the pianist brought to his remakes (especially his 1953 version with Krips – Decca ⊙ LXT2867, 4/54 – still awaiting reissue), the pianist's Apollonian poise stands as a convincing foil to the more assertive angularity of the 1949 Rubinstein/Golschmann/St Louis traversal (RCA ① 09026 61859-2), among other K488s of that era. Boyd Neel's buoyant, well-conceived leadership doesn't hurt either.

Curzon's mastery of Brahms's volatile D minor Concerto lies chiefly in his ability to reconcile Brahms's grieving lyricism and woolly thunderbolts without sectionalizing the music. Decca's *ffrr* sonics capture Curzon's wide dynamic range with a kind of impact that belies its vintage. I, for one, don't find it sonically inferior to the pianist's 1953 Concertgebouw/ van Beinum remake (Decca ① 421 143-2DH,

7/88). In contrast to the Dutch conductor's sturdy support and the warm, varnished tone of his orchestra, Jordá's shapeless, undisciplined podium work leaves his soloist largely to fend for himself. Chording is often imprecise and ill-tuned, while the first movement's tricky dotted rhythms emerge askew. There are also moments of ensemble slippage (for example, the sequence following the notorious double-octave cascade in the first movement, track 4 *c*11'00") that should have been remade. Still and all, Curzon's fiery outpourings in the outer movements contrast with his later, more restrained counterpart under Szell's authoritative baton (Decca ① 425 082-2DCS, 4/95).

Mike Dutton's transfers reveal more inner detail and less background noise than Roger Beardsley's restoration of the Mozart for Pearl (① GEM0027), although my suspicious ears perceive a soupçon of added reverberation in both CD editions. Curzon's admirers will find much to savour in this valuable reissue.

Jed Distler

Beethoven Piano Sonatas[a] – No. 8 in C minor, 'Pathétique', Op. 13; No. 14 in C sharp minor, 'Moonlight', Op. 27 No. 2; No. 21 in C, 'Waldstein', Op. 53.
Chopin 14 Waltzes[b]. Fantasie in F minor, Op. 49[b]. Berceuse in D flat, Op. 57[b].
Liszt Piano Sonata in B minor, S178[b]. La campanella, S141 No. 3[b]. Valse oubliée No. 1, S215. Sonetto 123 del Petrarca, S161 No. 6[b]. Etudes d'exécution transcendante, S139[b] – No. 5, Feux follets; No. 11, Harmonies du soir. [b]**Jeanne-Marie Darré,** [a]**Bruce Hungerford** (pfs).
Vanguard Classics ℗ ① 08.6597.73 (three discs: 190 minutes: ADD). From Vanguard originals, recorded 1965-7.

Vanguard's box, imprecisely entitled 'Romantic Piano Music', remembers on two of its three discs a great pianist in the later stages of her career (roughly after the time of her American début in 1962). Jeanne-Marie Darré, who recently died at the age of 93, was once described as a pianist in need of protection from her own vitality. A student of Isidor Philipp and Marguerite Long, she exemplified the French school of pianism at its most exuberant and scintillating. Celebrating her coming-of-age in style by performing all five Saint-Saëns concertos in a single concert, she left her outsize Paris audience exhilarated and pelted, as it were, with a ton of icing sugar. A stickler for technical perfection, she practised scales in octaves, thirds, fourths and sixths throughout her life and her results are spectacularly evident on VAI's two discs of early recordings dating from 1922-47 (VAIA/IPA ① VAIA1065-2). By her own admission Darré took time to deepen her art, to achieve greater breadth and inwardness, and her Liszt Sonata is as much a product of thoughtfulness as of rhetorical grandeur. Sadly shorn of its opening and vital bars on this transfer, it remains an interpretation of absorbing interest. Nothing is taken for granted, everything is experienced and savoured to the full and she rightly makes the central *Andante sostenuto* the spiritual centre of this unique romantic odyssey. There are bass reinforcements in the style of Horowitz but the fugue is surprisingly temperate for its *Allegro energico* marking and, overall, the sonata emerges in all its gravity, strength and scale, a landmark in the history of music.

In the shorter works Darré takes two of Liszt's most difficult *études* in her stride, opting for clarity rather than mere speed in *La campanella*, though never quite achieving a transition from *étude* to tone-poem in the ever-taxing *Feux follets* (something essentially for her early years). Again, she can be more voluble than expansive in *Harmonies du soir*, but in the *Sonetto 123 del Petrarca* she is as bold and inflammatory as she is lyrical.

Impeccable musicianship, underlined with an unmistakable touch of French rigour, is very much the order of the day in Darré's Chopin ('I like rhythm very much. I like people who play in time'). Yet her occasional severity is countered by a delectable sense of rhythmic play in the F major *Waltz*, and in the central *sostenuto* from the following A flat *Waltz* she breaks free of restraint, allowing herself a luxuriant sense of caprice. Her D flat *Minute Waltz* is graceful rather than hectic and time and again she surprises and delights you by easing from her celebrated *perlé* elegance into poetic reverie with the most patrician ease. Her *Fantasie*, too, puts paid to clichéd notions of French limitation, with playing ablaze with heroic strength as well as rare articulacy.

The inappropriateness of Vanguard's coupling is underlined by unexceptional performances.

All three of Bruce Hungerford's readings are fast-paced, offering little beyond the obvious, though there is a welcome touch of eloquence in the central section of the *Adagio* of the *Pathétique* Sonata.

Vanguard's presentation is weak (slender booklet-notes and neither biographical information nor recording dates) but their transfers are successful.   **Bryce Morrison**

· ·

Brüll Piano Concertos – No. 1 in F, Op. 10; No. 2 in C, Op. 24. Andante and Allegro, Op. 88. **Martin Roscoe** (pf); **BBC Scottish Symphony Orchestra / Martyn Brabbins.** Hyperion Ⓟ ① CDA67069 (73 minutes: DDD).

If Ignaz Brüll (1846-1907) is remembered at all, it's more for his cordial friendship with Brahms and Mahler than for his own qualities as a musician. But he was, by all accounts, a fine pianist (he partnered both Brahms and Mahler in two-piano performances of their symphonies) – and this latest disc in Hyperion's revelatory Romantic Piano Concerto series suggests that his compositions may not deserve their current neglect.

To be sure, on the basis of the three works here, it's hard to accept Brahms's assessment (a view also propounded in Hartmut Wecker's informative annotations) that Brüll had a knack for melody. While his themes tend to be distinctive (one of the features that makes his structures easy to follow), their melodic allure is limited: indeed, the identifying characteristic of the First Concerto's crucial opening theme is its almost interminable repetition of a single note. And even when his themes venture further, they're often so foursquare that they're worn through well before Brüll is finished with them, especially since his easygoing compositional style encourages him to meditate on them rather than to subject them to serious development. Nor was Brüll, despite his associations with Mahler, in any way a forward thinker. It's not surprising, of course, that his First Concerto filches as much as it does from Weber, Schumann and (especially in the rollicking finale) Mendelssohn: after all, the precocious composer was only 15 when he wrote it. But the *Andante and Allegro*, written more than 40 years later, inhabits much the same musical world.

Georgina Ivor Associates
present

Marc-André Hamelin
Exploration and Celebration

In the Master Series at the Wigmore Hall, London

Tuesday June 1st 1999
ALKAN Grande Sonate Op 33 *Les Quatres Ages*
MEDTNER Sonata Romantica in B flat minor Op 53 No 1
ECKHARDT-GRAMATTÉ Sonata No 6 *Drei Klavierstucke*

Tuesday June 8th 1999
MEDTNER Sonata in E minor Op 25 No 2 *Night Wind*
SCHUBERT Sonata in B flat major D960

Tuesday June 15th 1999
MEDTNER Sonate-Idylle in G Op 56
GODOWSKY Seven Studies after Chopin
RZEWSKI Variations on *The People United shall never be defeated*

Wigmore Hall Box Office: 0171 935 2141 Ticket prices: £16 £14 £12 £8
For further information about Marc-André Hamelin please contact
Georgina Ivor Associates tel: 0181 673 7179, fax: 0181 675 8058,
e-mail: GIvor@aol.com

Photo: Simon Perry / Hyperion

Still, if his harmonies are not especially adventurous, Brüll does deploy them with a tact that often adds a resonant warmth to his phrases. Then, too, there's an invigorating spring to his rhythms which, when combined with his generally transparent textures (rarely complicated by polyphonic sophistication) and his luminous (if never garish) orchestration, gives his music a refreshing lift. And while his concertos have enough athleticism to offer plenty of opportunity for the soloist to demonstrate his or her virtuosity, it's almost always dispatched with a smile.

In sum, the heroic striving that marks the Rubinstein concertos (much less the intellectual demands favoured by Brahms) does not seem to be high among Brüll's expressive priorities. His aspirations, at least on the basis of the music recorded here, are more light-hearted. And if these works never attain the inspired giddiness of the Moszkowski Concerto, they are never less than congenial. No surprise, then, that when he launches his 1868 Second Concerto with a tune redolent of the hunt, it turns out to herald a saunter through the country without a hint of violence.

One of the most astonishing characteristics of this series has been Hyperion's ability to find artists who can present obscure music with the confidence usually reserved for repertoire staples. This issue is no exception. Martin Roscoe darts through these scores with the same resilient rhythms and smartly defined gestures that gives his Dohnányi such authority (Hyperion ① CDA66684, 5/94) – and he's expertly supported by Martyn Brabbins and the BBC Scottish Symphony. Typically fine sound, too. **Peter J. Rabinowitz**

....

Chopin Scherzos – No. 1 in B minor, Op. 20; No. 2 in B flat minor, Op. 31; No. 3 in C sharp minor, Op. 39; No. 4 in E, Op. 54.
Ivo Pogorelich (pf).
DG Ⓟ ① 439 947-2GH (42 minutes: DDD).

It takes a remarkable amount of chutzpah for a pianist and record company to produce a full-price disc containing nothing but the four *Scherzos* of Chopin, even when they are stretched out to nearly 42 minutes. But this should not be surprising: only one of Pogorelich's DG recordings, in fact, exceeds an

hour's playing time and most are considerably under. The burning question, then, is whether Pogorelich here offers playing of such quality as to justify the expenditure.

These performances have inexplicably sat 'in the can' for the last three-and-a-half years and will probably appeal primarily to the pianist's followers, who are understandably eager to hear what Pogorelich does with three works that are new to his recorded repertoire. (A version of *Scherzo* No. 3 from 1981, carrying no major difference in approach, may be found on his début Chopin recital, DG ① 415 123-2GH, 5/85.) Pogorelich's interpretations are lean, dry and sparing of pedal. Owing to his extraordinarily *sec* tonal clarity, Pogorelich's pianistic command is never in doubt, nor is the absolute conviction lying behind his conceptions, no matter how unorthodox or misguided they may be. Pogorelich, it must be said, does adhere religiously to the actual notes of the scores – no left-hand octave doublings, no interlocking-octave rewrite at the‚end of *Scherzo* No. 1. None the less, there are too many liabilities here to allow any kind of general recommendation. A recurring mannerism of clipped, *staccato* phrase endings and unpleasantly chopped chords does no service to the music, and even more serious is the sectionalized nature of the pianist's interpretations; his inability or refusal to establish a basic tempo – not to mention a sequence of logical tempo relationships – slices each of the *Scherzos* into unrelated bits. One egregious example is the running passage that occurs twice (at 4'45" and 6'47") in *Scherzo* No. 2, where Pogorelich takes off like a rocket without relating the passage in any way to what precedes or follows it. Nor could the chorale-and-filigree alternations in No. 3 ever serve as a model of rhythmic precision. At other times he stretches out an interminable *rallentando* while the music wilts on the vine, and at about 7'30" into *Scherzo* No. 4 he practically grinds to a halt. Pogorelich's handling of the same work's opening is so wayward that if one were to attempt to notate rhythmically what he does, the result would bear no resemblance to Chopin's score.

As with most of this pianist's other recordings, the overall impression remains that of a powerful pianistic mechanism allied to an unusual musical mind, albeit one that does not choose – or perhaps possess the ability – to build large, convincing musical structures by sweeping

through them with unity as the objective. The recordings of the *Scherzos* by Rubinstein (RCA ① RD89651, 6/86), Wild (Chesky ① CD44), Katsaris (Teldec ① 4509-95499-2, 12/84^R) and Ashkenazy (Decca ① 417 474-2DH, 2/87) – all offering the four *Ballades* as well – are clearly to be preferred. DG's recorded sound is vivid and unimpeachable in every respect.

Donald Manildi

Chopin Concertos for Piano and Orchestra – No. 1 in E minor, Op. 11; No. 2 in F minor, Op. 21. **Martha Argerich (pf); Montreal Symphony Orchestra / Charles Dutoit.** EMI ℗ ① CDC5 56798-2 (69 minutes: DDD).

After a worryingly long break, Martha Argerich not long ago returned to the studio to set down on disc the Bartók Third and Prokofiev First and Third Concertos. That EMI issue was warmly welcomed in these pages by David Fanning (A/98); its successor, a coupling of the Chopin concertos with, once again, Dutoit and his Montreal orchestra, prompts me to praise even more impassioned.

These are quite magically beautiful performances. The qualities that have long made Argerich's Chopin special are abundantly in evidence – the astonishing technical brilliance; the directness, spontaneity and freedom of expression, subjective and 'plastic' to the nth degree yet profoundly in sympathy with the personality of composition and composer; the impetuous, sometimes breathtakingly volatile responses to lyrical caprice (aided by a natural, inimitably vivid command of rubato) and dramatic fantasy that nevertheless almost always unfold within the curve and flow of the musical argument; the extraordinarily vigorous rhythmic definition and volcanic urgency of attack, which combine to release a rush of blood in any dance-inspired music, any passage of *polonaise, mazurka* or *waltz* characterization; and, above all, the life-giving radiance of the sound world. Yet – and the point is strongly underlined by any reference to Argerich's previous recordings of these concertos – a new stillness and calm seem to have descended on her accounts of these works, a new inwardness; one feels in them a hitherto unsuspected blending of the 'personal' and the 'universal' Chopin that

makes the performances not just beautiful but moving to experience.

It is no doubt impertinent – and possibly sentimental as well – to speculate on whether Argerich's recent encounter with ill-health has anything to do with this development, or whether it is the inevitable consequence of the maturing process, the rethinking of interpretation on a level known only to the highest type of musical artistry. Whatever the reason, the alteration of viewpoint seems most startling in the F minor Concerto. The 1978 DG recording with Rostropovich and the National Symphony of Washington (currently available as part of the Concertos segment of DG's 'Martha Argerich Collection', ① 453 567-2GAC4, A/97) has proved to be one of the few disappointing items in the Argerich discography – forceful and at times exhilarating in its release of energies yet too seldom marked by sustained refinement of touch or delicacy of statement (the full-tilt, at times even rather blowzy orchestral support doesn't exactly help), and altogether somewhat undisciplined in its unfolding.

Two decades later, refinement and delicacy are the leitmotivs of the reading: pianist and conductor explore a much broader approach to tempo, a much more spacious canvas, and so in the *Larghetto*, centrepiece of the work as seldom in my experience, the tapering and tracing of the melodic line achieve miracles of grace, purity and poise. The darkening of the skies from bar 41, flagged by three magnificently graded *con forza* demisemiquaver plunges, is an incomparable Argerich moment, at once forceful and contained, and dramatically all of a piece with what came before and what comes afterwards. One looks to the 1935 Chopin Second of Cortot (admittedly a very different sort of Chopin pianist) for a similar attainment of poetic freedom and poetic authority (EMI ① CZS7 67359-2, 6/92); and while Cortot's conductor, Barbirolli, seems a touch fleeter in keeping in step with the imaginative enterprise of his soloist than does Dutoit, the Montreal orchestra offers some lovely playing, particularly the wind.

Argerich's 1968 Chopin First, with Abbado and the LSO, has by contrast long kept its place among the most highly-esteemed modern recordings of the work (on CD it can be found both in the above-mentioned 'Argerich Collection' of concertos and, alongside the same team's Liszt No. 1, in DG's The Originals series

① 449 719-2GOR). In spite of a surprising (because unremembered) amount of coarse delivery from the LSO brass, it keeps its place still – pianist and conductor were completely at one in youthful outlook, which tells in the hush of the 'Romance' no less than in the energy of the Rondo. But once again the 1998 perfor- mance achieves distillation, rarefaction of sentiment, breadth in the musical canvas to a degree simply unimaginable three decades earlier. To my mind, this new EMI CD has all the hallmarks of a Chopin classic. **Max Loppert**

Martha Argerich – The Legendary 1965 Recording

Chopin Piano Sonata No. 3 in B minor, Op. 58. Mazurkas – No. 36 in A minor, Op. 59 No. 1; No. 37 in A flat, Op. 59 No. 2; No. 38 in F sharp minor, Op. 59 No. 3. Nocturne No. 4 in F, Op. 15 No. 1. Polonaise No. 6 in A flat, 'Heroic', Op. 53. Scherzo No. 3 in C sharp minor, Op. 39. **Martha Argerich** (pf). EMI Ⓟ ① CDC5 56805-2 (52 minutes: ADD).

There can be few artists of the post-war generation whose all-too-rare appearances, both in public and on disc, are more eagerly anticipated or more keenly discussed than Martha Argerich. As in the cases of her fore- bears Teresa Carreño, Rosita Renard and Guiomar Novaës, Argerich's pianism is notable for its remarkable combination of seemingly effortless technical resource and temperamental volatility. For all the combustibility of the mixture, however, the vehemence of Argerich's playing is seldom exploited to the disadvantage of the extraordinary subtleties of her art. Moreover, despite the self-imposed limits she places on the repertory she performs, such is the spontaneity of her approach that each of her interpretations, no matter how familiar in broad outline, is characterized by a profusion of con- trasting details beneath the surface.

Even on the surface there are appreciable differences between Argerich's reading of the B minor Sonata here and her DG version made a short time after (① 447 430-2GOR, 6/95), not least in the omission of the first-movement repeat. Such a formal contraction can, of course, contribute to the momentum with which the

movement unfolds, especially in light of the opening statement and its retrograde appear- ance, whose transpositional reiterations, if not handled with sufficient colouristic imagination, may lend themselves to a sensation of develop- mental stasis, even allowing for the underlying rhythmic energy of the writing. Ironically, how- ever, Argerich seems to some extent to rein in the propulsive power for which she has been renowned, even at this stage in her career, appearing instead to be seeking at every turn to exploit a deeply-felt expressive lyricism to offset the febrile intensity of the most energetic figura- tional devices. There are, of course, still the trademark rhythmic hustlings, the sometimes fitful rubato which could prove perilously desta- bilizing in lesser hands, and even occasional smudging of detail, especially in the left hand. The performance, though, if not as compelling as her later one, has the virtue of allowing us a less hectic view of subsidiary elements within the music, which elsewhere can too often be over- whelmed by the sheer turbulence of the action. Where, perhaps, the interpretation fails quite to deliver is in the clarity with which the essential polyphonic structure of the music is projected. The evidence of Chopin's intense study of major treatises on counterpoint by Cherubini and Kastler, as well as the reverence in which he held Bach, is apparent throughout the sonata, even implicitly in the presentation of its opening gesture, whose unaccompanied outline seems to epitomize a philosophy in which an exhaustive treatment of the material takes precedence over the intrinsic qualities of the material itself. Such a high concentration of constituent elements and the closely structured manner of their manipulation by devices such as inversion and retrograde, as well as through complex tonal and temporal relationships, make a cohesive unity within movements and across the whole canvas difficult to achieve. In this respect Argerich is not entirely convincing, especially where the improvisational quality with which she projects prominent thematic lines within the structural framework is often achieved at the expense of simultaneous melodic enunciation and of clari- fying the inherent variational features by which the materials are linked. In short, despite the undeniable effectiveness of many passages in Argerich's finale, in which Chopin, significantly, steers away from such a rigorously contrapuntal approach, one misses the organic wholeness of Lipatti's performance (most recently on Philips ⊕ 456 892-2PM2, W/99), as well as the unswerving sense of direction shown by, say, Weissenberg (RCA ⊙ SB6743).

Having been awarded a special prize at the 1965 Warsaw Chopin Competition for her *mazurka* performances, it is perhaps not surprising that some of the most satisfying playing on the disc comes in Argerich's account of the Op. 59 set. There is a vulnerability as well as an affecting wistfulness about the playing which captures the elusiveness of the idiom, with its harmonic ambiguities and subtle rhythmic inflexions, with rare acuity. At the other end of the scale, the excitement she generates in the A flat *Polonaise*, and not simply in the left-hand octave section, is of an order that goes far beyond mere effect, its motivation derived from musical aspirations of compelling authority and total integrity.

Given the extraordinarily convoluted machinations behind the scenes which preceded the final release of these performances, we should be doubly grateful that they are now available for study. If they do not necessarily outstrip Argerich's other recordings of the same repertoire, they nevertheless offer an intriguing insight into ongoing 'work in progress' from a pianistic giant whose artistry continues to fascinate and, on occasion, perplex, more than 30 years later. **Charles Hopkins**

....

Chopin Piano Works. **Jon Nakamatsu** (pf). Harmonia Mundi ℗ ⊕ HMU90 7244 (69 minutes: DDD).
Impromptus – No. 1 in A flat, Op. 29; No. 2 in F sharp, Op. 36; No. 3 in G flat, Op. 51. Fantaisie-impromptu in C sharp minor, Op. 66. Fantasia on Polish Airs in A, Op. 13 (arr. Nakamatsu). Mazurkas – No. 36 in A minor, Op. 59 No. 1; No. 37 in A flat, Op. 59 No. 2; No. 38 in F sharp minor, Op. 59 No. 3. Berceuse in D flat, Op. 57. Polonaises – No. 1 in C sharp minor, Op. 26 No. 1; No. 3 in A, 'Military', Op. 40 No. 1; No. 6 in A flat, 'Heroic', Op. 53.

Jon Nakamatsu's Chopin recital follows Harmonia Mundi's release of his Gold Medal-winning performances in the 1997 Van Cliburn International Piano Competition (⊕ HMU90 7218, W/97). There, despite some reservations,

I found much to admire, though his Chopin (the Op. 22 *Andante spianato and Grande Polonaise brillante*) was arguably the least distinguished of his offerings. His new recital includes the Op. 13 *Fantasia on Polish Airs* heard, unusually, in the solo rather than piano-and-orchestra version, and here Nakamatsu is as characterful as he is pianistically fleet and elegant. Alas, such praise hardly extends to the rest of his programme which, despite much surface assurance, lacks the ease and flexibility of a truly patrician, high-born Chopin pianist. His *Berceuse* is prosaic in a sadly fashionable way and his Op. 59 *Mazurkas* (among the most finely-wrought examples of Chopin's genre) expose his cardinal failing, an insufficiently supple or resilient rhythm. He is slow off the mark, too, in the evergreen First *Impromptu*, its opening mordent more slack than vivacious, and although he strides more purposefully into the Second *Impromptu's* central march he shows too little sense of the music's underlying harmonic life and tension. True, the central *sostenuto* from the G flat *Impromptu* is more a case of melody and counter-melody than melody and accompaniment, yet the left hand's soaring 'cello' line should surely stand out in bolder relief. He takes a cautious rather than scintillating view of Chopin's *Allegro agitato* in the *Fantaisie-impromptu*, and the central *meno mosso* from the First *Polonaise* is notably staid. Impulse flags seriously in the central *energico fortissimo* from the A major *Polonaise* (almost as if the military had lost faith in their proud endeavour) and why such a coy withdrawal from the A flat *Polonaise's* heroic resonance (the principal theme on its first appearance)?

Competition enthusiasts should sample the Op. 13 *Fantasia*, but – this admirable exception apart – there is too little sense elsewhere of a pianist stylistically equal to his volatile and complex task. The recordings are adequate, but Chris Salocks's note, despite an amusing reminder that the A flat *Polonaise* (always among Chopin's most storming nationalist utterances) refers to three popular *Polonaises* (only the A major and A flat are universally familiar) and fails to mention that Chopin's 'commonplace harmonies' in the *Berceuse* are enlivened on the last page by one of his most audacious harmonic gestures. **Bryce Morrison**

Godowsky Passacaglia.
Schubert/Godowsky Rosamunde – Ballet music. 12 Songs. Moment musical No. 3.
Ian Hobson (pf).
Zephyr Ⓟ Ⓓ Z112-98 (69 minutes: DDD).

A decade ago only a handful of works by Godowsky had been recorded; today over 200 separate titles are available. It's a sad irony then that, with some notable exceptions, he has been poorly served in these recordings – especially when played by the 'completist' pianist (no names, no pack drill). Godowsky seems to attract either the literal, the incompetent or the uncomprehending.

Ian Hobson falls largely into the latter category. Here is a pianist who delights in adventurous programming (this one, the 'Complete Schubert/Godowsky', has been crying out to be done for years), is hugely knowledgeable about his art and instrument, and is mechanically well equipped. Yet Hobson's playing betrays little sense of poetry or affection for the music; he is unable to persuade us that, on the whole, composers have sound reasons (in both senses) for indicating where their music should be played *forte, piano, pianissimo* or *espressivo* (Godowsky might as well have been out walking the dog), or that charm, subtlety and a paint-box full of colours are just three prerequisites in playing Godowsky.

With the help of his sound engineer, Hobson's insistent tone hectors you from the very opening of *Rosamunde*, while Bolet (Decca Ⓓ 417 361-2DH, 7/87) is too slow but sings, and Hamelin (Musica Viva Ⓓ MVCD1026) skims detail but is witty. The 12 Schubert Songs, played in Schubert's chronological order of composition (not as published by Godowsky), are given a heavy-handed seeing to. Rarely is the spirit of Schubert glimpsed in these readings which seem to have been conceived as Regerian operatic paraphrases. Instead of fresh air, one is suffocated, so intent is Hobson on emphasizing Godowsky's labyrinthine textures. Carlo Grante gets closer (Music & Arts Ⓓ CD984) with playing of far more sophistication and imagination (Leopold Godowsky III, the composer's grandson, was his artistic adviser). Grante also finds a good deal more contrast and colour in the *Passacaglia* (44 variations, cadenza and fugue on the opening eight bars of Schubert's *Unfinished* Symphony), is over three minutes faster than Hobson and is only surpassed by Rian de Waal (Hyperion Ⓓ CDA66496, 3/92) and Hamelin, whose Musica Viva recording from 1987 remains the most impressive all-Godowsky recital on disc.

Try as I might to empathize with Hobson's approach and welcome his initiative, in the end it takes just the two minutes of Josef Hofmann (dedicatee of the Schubert Songs in their collected edition) playing the *Moment musical* No. 3 (Marston Ⓓ 52014-2, reviewed on page 99) to demonstrate the huge gap between Hobson and Godowsky.   **Jeremy Nicholas**

Nadia Reisenberg – The Acclaimed Haydn Recordings

Nadia Reisenberg (pf). Ivory Classics mono Ⓜ Ⓓ 70806 (two discs: 148 minutes: ADD). Items marked [a] from Westminster XWN18357, [b]XWN18356, [c]XWN18057. Recorded 1955-6 and 1958. **Haydn:** Piano Sonatas – No. 13 in G, HobXVI/6[a]; No. 35 in A flat, HobXVI/43[b]; No. 50 in D, HobXVI/37[a]; No. 53 in E minor, HobXVI/34[d]; No. 60 in C, HobXVI/50[b]; No. 62 in E flat, HobXVI/52[a]; F minor, HobXVII/6[c]. Fantasia in C, HobXVII/4[c]. Six Variations in C, HobXVII/5[c]. 20 Variations in A, HobXVII/2[c]. Capriccio in G, HobXVII/1[c]. Variations in E flat, HobXVII/3[c].

Nadia Reisenberg (born Vilnius, Lithuania, 1904; died New York City, 1983) initially studied at the St Petersburg Conservatory under Leonid Nikolayev (who also taught Shostakovich and Sofronitsky), before leaving Russia, making a successful series of débuts in central Europe and then moving to the United States in 1922. There, she continued her studies with Alexander Lambert, as well as with Josef Hofmann at the Curtis Institute where she subsequently joined the faculty. Among the most remarkable of her achievements was the performance of the complete Mozart piano concerto canon in a series of radio broadcasts in 1938-9. I recall their conductor, the late Alfred Wallenstein, telling me how impressive those performances were. In her later years, Reisenberg was a venerated faculty member of New York's Juilliard School.

These discs were extremely well received at the time of their release in the 1950s on Westminster, a period when Haydn's keyboard music on record was still a relatively rare commodity except for some of the more popular late sonatas and, of course, the great F minor Variations. Since that time, of course, there have been anthologies of more than just single-disc collections by such performers as Landowska (harpsichord and piano, released shortly after her death in 1959 – RCA Victor ⊙ LM6073), Artur Balsam on L'Oiseau-Lyre (⊙ SOL273/5), Gilbert Kalish on five separately issued Nonesuch LPs, the admirable John McCabe with a ground-breaking complete set on Decca from the mid-1970s (① 443 785-2LC12, 12/95), Jenö Jandó (on seven separately issued Naxos CDs) and, most recently, András Schiff (see opposite). Neither should one discount such other important sometime Haydn players as Horowitz, Richter, Brendel and Glenn Gould. Period-instrument performances have also proliferated through such names as Fritz Neumeyer, Badura-Skoda, Lola Odiaga, and, as I understand it, a promised integral recording is forthcoming from Alan Curtis.

How does this 40-year-old Reisenberg recording stand up to what may now be considered substantial competition? In matters of textual accuracy (the Christa Landon edition had not yet appeared) or the most recent pronouncements on such stylistic matters as ornamentation or overdotting where required, these performances may not be quite up to date, but these are details that do not really interfere with the basic highly musical qualities of her interpretations. Reisenberg, to her great credit, did not romanticize or overdramatize Haydn. Nor were her dynamics ever exaggerated as one so often hears on the modern instrument. This is sensitive, expressive playing, classically eloquent where needed (as in the F minor Variations or the slow movements of Nos. 53 and 60) and often sparkling in fast movements. Technically, too, all is on the highest level, with exceptionally well-balanced voicing and careful, never smudged, articulation. Though one may imagine more of Haydn's graphic humour being conveyed in, for example, the Sauschneider *Capriccio* (based on the Austrian folk-song, *It takes eight of you to castrate a male pig*), including the poor animal scampering off at the end, her well-defined lyrical shaping gives much pleasure.

A comparison of the original Westminster LPs with the CD reissues reveals that, other than

a slight top cut and an equally small bass boost, the intimate sound of the piano in the relatively but not oppressively dry Esoteric Studios in New York is natural though not especially colourful. Overall, these are performances that will effectively stand up to comparison with the majority of other available Haydn keyboard recordings. One might hope that Ivory Classics will look to her Tchaikovsky, Rachmaninov and Kabalevsky recordings for future reissue as well.

Igor Kipnis

Haydn Piano Sonatas. **András Schiff** (pf).
Teldec ℗ ① 0630-17141-2 (two discs:
147 minutes: DDD).
No. 32 in G minor, HobXVI/44; No. 33
in C minor, HobXVI/20; No. 53 in E minor,
HobXVI/34; No. 54 in G, HobXVI/40;
No. 58 in C, HobXVI/48; No. 59 in E flat,
HobXVI/49; No. 60 in C, HobXVI/50;
No. 61 in D, HobXVI/51; No. 62 in E flat,
HobXVI/52. Fantasia in C, HobXVII/4.

András Schiff adds to his many laurels with a splendid Haydn collection of mostly late works, played with a fine combination of drama and genial charm. Character and personality, as well as dazzling technical brilliance, are evident throughout. The rhythms are rock solid, but one also savours the warmth of his subtle rubato. Pedalling is spare but far from dry and the dynamic range, with wonderful *pianissimos*, is wide but seldom exaggerated. The minor-key sonatas emerge with commendable seriousness, yet with emotions that still remain largely classical (the finale of No. 33, for instance), and Haydn's often quirky humour, with its sudden surprises, is both scintillatingly and appropriately conveyed.

From a performance-practice standpoint, these intelligently-conceived readings stand out for such details as ornamentation, dynamics and articulation, although one could occasionally complain about unobserved *staccato* wedges and a rather conservative attitude towards added embellishments, one particular area he espouses in his written Forward to the set. Quite admirable is the pianist's treatment of Haydn's amazing *fermata* pauses, in which Schiff will daringly wait for as long as 13 seconds before continuing (for example, the *Fantasia* in C at 3'59" or in the first movement of Sonata No. 62).

I would have no hesitation in recommending this as some of the very best keyboard Haydn to be found on record, and that applies as well to the superb piano reproduction.

The excellent booklet contains detailed annotations about the sonatas by Misha Donat, but the real eye-opener is the introduction by Schiff himself, 'Haydn's Piano Sonatas – A Short History of their Reception and Interpretation'. The pianist hurls some surprising brickbats, not only at other pianists who have performed Haydn but even at some listeners. A few quotes may serve to illustrate: 'Sviatoslav Richter, one of the greatest artists, played a lot of Haydn, but I do not think he contributes greatly to our understanding of the composer. Nor is Haydn among Richter's strongest performances. (Russian culture and Viennese classicism are very remote from each other, and it is quite absurd how people in the West are fascinated by Russian musicians' maltreatment of the classics.)' Schiff considers Glenn Gould's six Haydn sonatas recording (Sony Classical ℗ SM2K52623, 1/95) to be 'to put it mildly, very strange indeed ... Gould was a brilliant musician and pianist who, thanks to his Bach recordings, his rather unconventional views on musical and other matters and, finally, his untimely death, has reached the status of a cult figure ... This is dangerous if the admiring fans and critics are unable to distinguish the true achievements from the parodies. Gould's Haydn is just as bizarre and perverted as his Mozart; it shows a complete ignorance of the classical style and as such can be appreciated only by similarly ignorant listeners.' There is more, but the message is clear. Were Schiff not such a marvellous performer, one would call such comments impertinent and inappropriate, but, startling as his remarks are, one cannot help but admire his forthrightness. One wonders how others will respond to such candour.　　**Igor Kipnis**

Liszt Complete Piano Music, Volumes 53a and 53b. **Leslie Howard** (pf); **Budapest Symphony Orchestra / Karl Anton Rickenbacher.**
Hyperion ℗ ① CDA67401/2 and CDA67403/4 (two sets of two discs, oas: 158 and 175 minutes: DDD).
CDA67401/2: Concertos for Piano and Orchestra – No. 1 in E flat, S124; E flat,

S125a (ed. Rosenblatt/Howard). Fantaisie on a theme from Beethoven's 'Ruinen von Athen', S122. Totentanz, S126 (final version). Grande fantaisie symphonique on themes from Berlioz's 'Lélio', S120. Malédiction, S121. Grand Solo de Concert, S365. Hexaméron – Morceau de concert, S365b. Polonaise brillante, S367.
CDA67403/4: Concerto for Piano and Orchestra No. 2 in A, S125. De profundis, S691 (ed. Rosenblatt/Howard). Wanderer Fantasy, S366. Concerto pathétique in E minor, S365a. Konzertstück in F minor, S367a. Totentanz, S126i (1849 version, arr. Busoni). Fantasia on Hungarian Folk Themes, S123. **?Liszt/Menter:** Ungarische Zigeunerweisen, S714 (orch. Tchaikovsky).

The 17 works presented in these two volumes constitute the most complete collection of Liszt's works for piano and orchestra that is ever likely to appear. By contrast, Michel Béroff's similarly titled release from the late 1970s (EMI ① CZS7 67214-2, 1/81[R]) contained only nine works. Leslie Howard has put a great deal of effort and research into the preparation of these discs, and for this he is to be commended. *De profundis*, for example, required that Howard add six bars in order to complete the work; in the *Hexaméron*, Howard not only had to reconstruct the work from manuscript sources, but also orchestrate certain sections; the *Grand Solo de Concert* is another work that required reconstruction, while, in several other works, careful study of the manuscripts led to many corrections. All of this is disclosed in Howard's exemplary notes, along with brief but detailed analyses and histories of each work.

From an academic viewpoint these are very noteworthy releases. The problem, however, is that much of the playing could also best be described as academic. The works presented range from the very familiar to the completely unknown; at least four here receive their first recording and, aside from the two well-known concertos, *Totentanz* and the *Fantasia on Hungarian Folk Themes*, the remaining pieces have each been recorded a handful of times at most. Although it is the lesser-known works that will be of greatest interest to potential buyers, some comments still need to be made about the more famous ones, most of which receive substandard performances. The First Concerto is given a particularly dull reading that is probably the low point of the set; although the Second Concerto fares somewhat better, its opening is again disconcertingly flat. Perhaps the existence of so many top-rank performances of these works adds unfairly to the negative impression. *Totentanz* appears in both its first version and its more familiar second. The manuscript of Liszt's first version was not made available for study by its owner, thus Busoni's edition had to serve as the source. While the earlier version shares much material with the later one (although in a more primitive state), there is also some quite beautiful music in the latter part of the first version that is not present in the second, including Liszt's utilization of the *De profundis* theme. Howard is not the first performer to investigate this earlier version of *Totentanz*; Raymond Lewenthal made an arrangement in the 1960s in which he combined the two versions using what he considered the best parts of both (Columbia ☉ MS7252). He coyly described the result as Liszt/Lewenthal, while readily admitting that there was not a single note of Lewenthal in it.

For the most part, the works based on pieces by other composers receive fairly straightforward performances. The Weber *Polonaise brillante* comes off relatively well, with Howard injecting some vigour into the dance rhythms, and the *Fantaisie on a theme from Beethoven's 'Ruinen von Athen'* also receives energetic treatment. The Schubert *Wanderer Fantasy*, on the other hand, is far too rigid and earthbound. The *Grande fantaisie symphonique*, a large-scale work based on Berlioz's *Lélio*, is generally well played, although a number of the octave sections are lacking in direction and some of the passagework seems to lack focus; in spite of these lapses of concentration, however, Howard's performance leaves one convinced that the work deserves to be heard more often.

Of the remaining works, the posthumously published Concerto in E flat and the *Grand Solo de Concert* are both persuasively played. The latter is an immediately appealing piece – we must be grateful to Howard for his painstaking work in its reconstruction – and is played with considerable flair. On the other hand, his reading of *De profundis*, Liszt's largest concerted work, is simply too mundane to hold one's concentration over the required time-span. The second set includes a bonus disc of the work by

Sophie Menter, although it is uncertain whether Liszt assisted in its composition. Still, it is an attractive work that bears strong thematic resemblance to some of Liszt's own *Hungarian Rhapsodies*.

Those selectively choosing which volumes to buy in this series will have to give these discs serious consideration. Granted, the playing is desperately uneven, but it is far from incompetent. Howard never brings one to the edge of one's seat, nor does he captivate with exquisitely turned phrases, but he does give scholarly renditions that are faithful to the score, and he has the technique to play these pieces in a competent manner. One can prefer Ginzburg (Arlecchino ① ARL190) and Bolet (Opus ☉ MLG81) in the *Ruinen von Athen Fantaisie*, Bolet (Decca ① 425 689-2DX, 2/90) in the *Wanderer Fantasy*, Frith (Naxos ① 8 550959) or Béroff (EMI ① CZS5 69662-2, 1/81[R]) in the Weber *Polonaise brillante* and numerous others in the two concertos and *Fantasia on Hungarian Folk Themes*, but such comparisons are beside the point since the main reason to own these sets is to have a complete representation of Liszt's *oeuvre* for piano and orchestra, even if the performances are far from world-class.   **Farhan Malik**

....

Maria Yudina, Volume 1.
Mozart Concertos for Piano and Orchestra –
  No. 20 in D minor, K466[a]; No. 23 in A,
  K488[b]. Piano Sonata No. 14 in C minor,
  K457 – Allegro assai[c]. **Maria Yudina** (pf);
  [a]**USSR Radio Symphony Orchestra / Sergei
  Gorchakov;** [b]**Moscow Radio Symphony
  Orchestra / Alexander Gaouk.**
  Dante mono Ⓔ ① HPC121 (60 minutes:
  ADD). Item marked [b] from (USSR)
  014983/9, [c](USSR) 014990. All items
  recorded 1948.

Maria Yudina, Volume 2.
Beethoven Concerto for Piano and Orchestra
  No. 4 in G, Op. 58[a]. Fantasia for Piano,
  Chorus and Orchestra in C minor, Op. 80[b].
  Maria Yudina (pf); [a]**Leningrad Philharmonic
  Orchestra / Kurt Sanderling;** [b]**USSR Radio
  Chorus and Symphony Orchestra / Sergei
  Gorchakov.**
  Dante mono Ⓔ ① HPC122 (54 minutes:
  ADD). Item marked [a] recorded in Leningrad
  in 1947, [b]Moscow in 1948.

Maria Yudina, Volume 3.
Brahms 25 Variations and Fugue on a Theme
by G. F. Handel, Op. 24[a].
Schubert Piano Sonata No. 21 in B flat,
D960[b]. **Maria Yudina** (pf).
Dante mono ℗ ① HPC123 (66 minutes:
ADD). Item marked [a] recorded in Moscow
in 1948, [b]Moscow in 1947.

Of all the many legendary pianists from the
former Soviet Union, Maria Yudina has a good
claim to being the most legendary of all: at least
in the sense that the stories about her are the
most extraordinary, while opportunities to
experience her playing in the West have been
minimal. Fearless, fervently religious and utterly
unmaterialistic, in a society ruled by fear and
(nominally at least) by anti-religious material-
ism, she was looked upon by her devoted
audiences as much more than a pianist (to adapt
Yevtushenko's famous description of Russian
poets). Yet, like Sofronitsky – with whom she
and Shostakovich studied in Leonid Nikolayev's
Petrograd Conservatoire class from 1920 – she
was never allowed to travel to the West, and few
of her many recordings ever circulated on
Western labels. So we're left with vivid descriptions – of an ascetic, unworldly figure in a floor-
length black dress, with hands like eagle's claws
(according to the Shostakovich of Volkov's
Testimony: Hamish Hamilton; 1979) – but it's up
to us to re-create the aura that reportedly
surrounded her performances.

That's not always so easy to do. These three
Dante issues are taken from 1947-8 Russian
recordings. The sound has been partially
cleaned up but remains on the whole pretty
fuzzy, and in almost every piece the instrument
soon becomes seriously detuned in the treble.
Edits tend to come very audibly on structural
joins, and in at least two instances whole phrases
have been snipped out (the first movement of the
Beethoven concerto at 8'13", bars 212-15; the
finale of the Schubert sonata at 4'27", bars 360-
9). Admittedly Yudina could certainly play fast
and loose with the text, and she got flak for it
from Shostakovich and Neuhaus among others:
sudden *meno mossos* and agogic distortions
were very much her style, and she wasn't above
deleting or even adding repeats (hear the
opening of the Schubert third movement!). But
I can't see her idiosyncrasies extending to those
particular excisions.

Readers of *IPQ* will be well used to filtering out
the distractions of early recordings and listening
for the spirit behind the notes. So I'm happy to
report that there's at least one performance on
these discs which enshrines Yudina's spirit, and
in all the others there are moments which do
credit to her unique personality.

In the Mozart D minor Concerto such
moments are few and far between, however.
After a wonderfully eloquent first solo, the
Allegro soon becomes merely expression by
numbers, a succession of predictable agogic
tricks. The slow movement shows how narrow
the line can be between merely pedestrian phrasing (the opening solo) and lofty simplicity (the
first episode); Beethoven's cadenza is the highlight of an otherwise peremptory account of the
finale. The A major Concerto is apparently the
recording made at Stalin's behest (as memorably
described in *Testimony*). Listening to it in that
light it's hard not to experience a certain *frisson*,
though the actual playing is again a disconcert-
ing mixture of elevated moments and extended
passages of, frankly, dullness.

Jean-Charles Hoffelé's claim that Yudina's
Beethoven 'seems to harbour a new truth that
no Western pianist has ever seen in it' is the sort
of pious nonsense that gets booklet-note writers
a bad name. In fact Yudina gives a generally
sub-standard account of the G major Concerto:
prosaic and didactic in the first movement,
mannered in the second, rushed and technically
shoddy in the third. One redeeming feature is
her nicely exploratory playing of the rarely
heard Brahms cadenzas. The *Choral Fantasia* is
sturdy and sensible, while the rustic woodwind
and carefully rehearsed chorus, singing in
Russian, are at least interesting from the point of
view of historic performance practice.

For me the one interpretation which comes
closest to living up to the Yudina legend is her
Schubert B flat Sonata. She begins the first
movement even more slowly than Richter
(Music & Arts ① CD642), but soon swings from
this to the opposite extreme of dramatic immediacy. It's a volatile reading, at one moment brittle and severe, at the next as smooth as silk. The
development section is an astonishing inward
journey, which had me hanging on every note.
Technically virtually everything in this movement, bar the lumpy bass trills, manages to
stand up to the intense emotional strain of the
interpretation. Hear the broken-heartedness of

the opening theme at the recapitulation and you realize, perhaps, where Yudina's glacial opening tempo comes from.

It's reported that she saw Bach's *Goldberg Variations* as a series of illustrations to the Bible. I can't say that that came across to me hearing her recording of the piece in the Philips series (① 456 994-2PM2); but such is the stricken tone she finds for the beginning of Schubert's slow movement I wonder if she didn't have in mind the ultimate biblical expression of despair at that point: 'My God, my God, why hast Thou forsaken me?'. Once again she wears her spirituality on her sleeve, yet juxtaposes this with an almost excessive severity. The *Scherzo* struck me as comparatively unremarkable. But the finale is another compelling experience, often quirkily spasmodic, like a Schumann *Novelette* delivered by a highly caffeinated Florestan.

Only slightly less remarkable are the Brahms Variations: noble, deft and poetic playing, with some wonderful touches of caprice (two very distinct tempos for Var. 12, for instance), abundant rhythmic, wilful distortions (Vars. 3 and 17), plus a masochistic avoidance of pedal in the *legato* octaves of Var. 6 and a wonderfully bold summons in Var. 9 – 'Veni creator spiritus'?

David Fanning

....

Poulenc Complete Solo Piano Works.
Eric LeSage (pf).
RCA Red Seal Ⓔ ① 74321 63214-2
(three discs, 206 minutes: DDD). Currently only available from retailers in France.
Presto in B flat. Mouvements perpétuels. Mélancolie. Les soirées de Nazelles. Humoresque. Suite. Pastourelle. Le bal masqué – Intermède in D minor. Trois novelettes. Trois pièces. Bourrée, au pavillon d'Auvergne. 15 Improvisations. Badinage. Trois intermezzos. Napoli. Suite Française d'après Claude Gervaise. Valse-improvisation sur le nom de Bach. Feuillets d'album. Cinq impromptus. Thème varié. Valse. Pièce brève sur le nom d'Albert Roussel. Nocturnes. Villageoises. Promenades. L'histoire de Babar, le petit éléphant (with Frédéric Lodéon, narr)[a].

After Debussy and Ravel, and before Messiaen, Poulenc's is the most significant body of French solo piano music of the twentieth century, even

if, in overall artistic merit, it falls some way short of that of his illustrious predecessors. Whilst Poulenc composed a relatively large amount for the piano, a reasonable proportion of this music is somewhat lightweight, a fact which should deter many from listening to over three hours of it in one sitting.

None the less, any musical person will respond to the warmly Gallic wit and limpid expression of this naturally gifted composer. Poulenc's work is inherently and unfailingly musical – and as he was also a gifted pianist, his piano writing stems from a genuine understanding of the instrument, being gratefully written for the executant.

Poulenc was born in January 1899, and his centenary is notably commemorated by various new sets and reissues. One might hope that before the end of the year those companies – particularly Sony – who possess recordings by the composer himself will have reissued them (in the interim, collectors are directed to the Pearl disc 'Poulenc d'après Poulenc' ① GEMMCD9311, 10/88), but in the meantime we have Eric LeSage's new RCA box, claiming to be Poulenc's 'Complete Music for Solo Piano' on three CDs, which, unfortunately, is not quite complete.

Many collectors may be satisfied with LeSage, but they are cautioned that his performances are variable, the recording – as so often with RCA in solo piano music – is not the finest one can imagine, and the instrument itself is curiously inconsistent in timbre, especially in the top register. As indicated earlier, this collection is not as complete as it should be. Missing are the 'Caprice' from *Le bal masqué* – the 'Intermède' from the same score is here – and the two items in Poulenc's own transcription from *Les Biches*: 'Adagietto' and 'Rondo', which the composer himself recorded (they are on the Pearl CD, together with the 'Caprice'). Also omitted are the early *Trois pastorales*, of which Decca's Pascal Rogé set (almost identical in repertoire, ① 460 598-2DM3) claims the world première recording, although LeSage includes (as does Rogé) the recomposed version of the first two of these pieces, as well as a new third piece under the title of *Trois Pièces*. In addition, and strictly speaking, the piano-duet Sonata of 1918 is also a work for solo piano which is not in either set. Finally, despite Frédéric Lodéon's elegant recitation, *L'histoire de Babar* is quite unnecessary in LeSage's collection; the more so in view of the missing items.

Technically, LeSage almost has it all. In the superbly written *Improvisations* – the best playing on the records, and arguably the finest music – he is admirable, but his spreading of the left-hand tenths in the *Presto* in B flat major, compared with, say, Horowitz's recording (for whom the piece was written – most recently available on APR ⊙ APR5517, 5/98), appears exaggerated to the point where the piece begins to suffer. None the less, LeSage is a very clean and accomplished player, and it is unlikely that one would find anyone today who is superior in this regard. Unfortunately, he is by no means so admirable in his sensitivity and response to the music. The overriding impression remains of a pianist who, for all his technical ability, is not wholly involved; nor does he appear to have this music completely within his re-creative psyche – all the notes are here, but in comparison with Poulenc's own recordings, for all of their splashes of sustaining pedal to cover the really difficult bits, the elements of fantasy and imagination are but intermittently conveyed by LeSage. The most critical observation as regards his playing is his frequent lack of dynamic contrast – rather too much of this music is played at a virtually unvaried *mezzo-forte*, and whilst there is some vindication for this in the *Mouvements perpétuels*, the almost total lack of genuine poetry conveyed by such an approach inevitably detracts from the music itself.

The recording reveals that, basically, the microphone placing for the instrument is surely wrong. The sound of the Steinway D is at times distant and reverberant, betraying the engineer's inability to master fully the empty hall. This is more apparent on large playback set-ups, where the sound tends to muddy the texture. Through small equipment the sound works better, and on good-quality headphones it is better still. However, little can be done to correct the imbalance of the instrument itself, when the quality of timbre in its high register is at times inconsistent from take to take and at variance with the lower keyboard region.

LeSage's set comes up against direct competition from Pascal Rogé's Decca box. Rogé's recordings were made over 12 years in London and Paris in three venues, with three pianos, three producers and three sets of engineers, yet the differences in sound are not significant, and,

overall, Decca's piano quality, whilst never reaching demonstration standard, is preferable to RCA's. These CDs have, of course, already garnered enthusiastic reviews, with which, by and large, I concur.

Rogé may not, in the last analysis, have quite the steely articulation of LeSage, but in sheerly musical terms he is often preferable. In short, he is a more refined and finished artist than LeSage. A case in point is the *Presto*, which Rogé takes slightly more slowly: at first, LeSage is more exciting, and his ending is more humorous, but Rogé is far more musical in terms of phrasing and characterization in the central section, where LeSage appears uninterested and purely mechanical. The latter scores heavily in that he has recorded the 15 *Improvisations* complete, whereas Rogé took three years and two discs to finish the set, and whilst they should not be regarded as an indivisible work, they gain much from being heard in sequence. This piece also demonstrates LeSage's very best playing.

Notwithstanding the excitement that LeSage conveys, and Rogé's appealing finesse, in terms of the best available realization on disc of Poulenc's music, the five-disc EMI set is really the one to have (⊙ CMS5 66831-2, 1/99). In the first place, it offers virtually the same solo piano music as both RCA and Decca – with one or two similar omissions – but it also includes the complete music for two pianists, at one and two pianos, as well as Poulenc's complete published chamber music. If some may balk at not having the solo piano music played by one artist – here, it is shared by Gabriel Tacchino and Jacques Février, and recorded over a far longer period, 1966-85 – these two artists knew Poulenc intimately, and the recordings still sound excellent and quite natural. Apart from anything else, they each play with an indefinable quality, a mixture of love and authority, which is so compelling that I found myself returning to the EMI set again and again. In the music for two pianists, Tacchino and Février are simply wonderful. Except for the Violin Sonata (with Frank Peter Zimmermann and Alexander Lonquich) and the brief *Bagatelle* for violin and piano (David Grimal and Emanuel Strosser), Février is the pianist in all the other chamber works, accompanying such artists as Pierre Fournier, Maurice Bourgue, Michel Debost and Alan Civil in exemplary performances. Clearly, with recordings that date back over 30 years, one cannot expect the finest in sound – but, seriously, have we progressed that much since then? Surely the purpose of recording is to serve the performer, and the purpose of the performer is to serve the composer. Despite such imperfections as occasional drop-out in the left-hand channel in the *Valse* in C major, and other minor flaws – in reality, very few – the EMI set has a consistency of musicianship which reveals the essence of Poulenc's music in a manner which Rogé, for all his admirable qualities, does not quite manage, and LeSage, on this showing, cannot fully approach. However, one should add that the splendid suite *Les soirées de Nazelles* is played by Jacques Février in the composer's revised version, wherein Variations 4-6 were suppressed: both Rogé and LeSage play the work in the original complete version.

In terms of presentation, Decca merely reboxes the three single CDs, with the original individual booklet-notes for Vols. 1 and 2 and a far better one for the latest disc; RCA has much more detailed booklets for each CD, and EMI has a separate 64-page booklet, with more photographs. A nice touch from EMI is that each of the five CDs is adorned with a different signature by the composer. If you merely want the solo piano music, then the choice between LeSage and Rogé is not entirely clear-cut: on balance, the Decca set is to be preferred, but LeSage is often very exciting. However, I have no doubt that the EMI collection will give the most lasting musical satisfaction of all.

Robert Matthew-Walker

Reger Variations and Fugue on a theme of J. S. Bach, Op. 81. Variations and Fugue on a theme of Telemann, Op. 134. Five Humoresques, Op. 20. **Marc-André Hamelin** (pf). Hyperion Ⓟ Ⓒ CDA66996 (74 minutes: DDD).

The short-lived yet frighteningly prolific Max Reger casts his irascible shadow over the fringes of the late romantic/early twentieth-century repertoire. Reger's detractors view him as a crusty beacon of the rearguard, carting overstuffed wares uphill along a dead-end avenue. His acolytes, on the other hand, have stared fashion in the eye and beat the Regerian drum without shame. Rudolf Serkin must have caught

his fans (and record company, no doubt) offguard when he recorded the Piano Concerto (CBS ⊙ SBRG72399, 6/66) and, late in his life, the *Variations and Fugue on a theme of J. S. Bach* (CBS Ⓒ MK39562, 1/87). Claudio Arrau also wanted to record the latter, but never did, while Jorge Bolet essayed Reger's *Telemann* Variations for Decca (Ⓒ 417 791-2DM, 11/81R).

More musicians are turning to Reger on disc, and it was only a matter of time before Marc-André Hamelin wrapped his hands around the variation sets, adding the *Humoresques* for good measure. If Reger's piano music lies off the beaten track and contains more notes than the Bank of England, you can rest assured that the pied piper called Hamelin will come a-calling. Superlatives are dangerous, but if I ventured to say that Hamelin is arguably the most proficient pianist alive, few would disagree. He commands Reger's dense textures, Crisco-thick contrapuntal labyrinths, treacherous registral leaps and lightning scale-passages with effortless aplomb. What's more, he never makes an ugly sound. Gnarly chordal sequences are always voiced in full, with no hint of splintering, as are Hamelin's ricocheting octaves. What instantly identifies his sound are the rapid, rolled chords, emerging from the bass register like a hungry shark.

The pianist, to be sure, does not betray the music's darker sides, nor point up the harmonic or polyphonic tension lurking underneath Reger's elaborate upholstery. That's not his way. In the slower, more introspective movements of the *Bach* Variations, for example, András Schiff's horizontal approach (Teldec Ⓒ 4509-99051-2, 11/95) pays profounder dividends, while trills and turns take on a melodic urgency absent from Hamelin's decorative dispatch. When it comes down to the nuts and bolts, however, Schiff's somewhat unreliable double-note technique yields to Hamelin's unruffled security.

Reger's *Five Humoresques* reveal the composer's lighter side, yet Hamelin's po-faced demeanour doesn't allow the music's earthy charm and Magyar-tinged syntax to come through as it might. At any rate, Hyperion's recording captures Hamelin's sonority with gorgeous realism. Rob Cowan's perceptive notes make an interesting and cogent case for Reger as the missing link between Brahms and Bruckner – though I'll have to sleep on that argument, and won't be giving you an answer in the morning!

Jed Distler

Saint-Saëns Etudes – Op. 52; Op. 111.
Etudes for the left-hand, Op. 135. Thème
varié, Op. 97. **Piers Lane** (pf).
Hyperion Ⓟ Ⓒ CDA67037 (72 minutes:
DDD).

Alfred Cortot expressed it well when he wrote
(in *La musique française de piano*; Paris: 1930)
that Saint-Saëns 'accepts the piano for what it is,
with its short-sounding timbre and percussive
qualities. He dreads the fallacious delusion of
the pedals, the uncanny witchcraft of mingled
harmonies, the languors of touch, and what he
calls "the mania for expressive playing and
monotonous legato".' This was undoubtedly
Cortot's diplomatic way of saying that what
Saint-Saëns disliked in piano playing was what
Cortot sought hardest to achieve. So it is ironic
that two of the most memorable early recordings
of Saint-Saëns's piano music are the ones Cortot
made of the Fourth Concerto (Pearl Ⓒ
GEMMCD9491) and the 'Etude en forme de
valse' from Op. 52 (Biddulph Ⓒ LHW014/5,
10/94). Cortot was capable of the fast, dry,
shallow style known as the *jeu perlé* which
Saint-Saëns had inherited from his teacher
Stamaty, but of course he was among the first
French pianists to go well beyond that.

The *Etudes* of Saint-Saëns, composed between
1877 and 1912, look neither back to Chopin nor
ahead to Debussy – to choose the two major
composers whose *Etudes* reflect a concern with
pedal, touch and expressiveness. In Op. 52,
formulas and pretty turns of phrases abound,
with few pianistically original ideas until the
final 'Etude en forme de valse' – which is as brilliant a test of double-notes as it is of style. The
finest recordings of this *étude* include those by
Cortot (listed above), Darré (Art et Musique
⊙ MA103/8007 – nla), Tagliaferro (Philips Ⓒ
438-959-2PM3), Cziffra (APR Ⓒ APR5554) and
Duchâble (EMI Ⓒ CES5 72356-2).

Op. 111 is a set of greater pianistic interest,
and its *Etudes* in thirds and chromatics continue
to have a certain pedagogic value today. But, like
Op. 52, it contains only one real masterpiece, the
final 'Toccata'. This *tour de force* has been
stunningly recorded twice by Darré (the first,
from 1931, is available on VAI Ⓒ VAI1065-2),
Duchâble (details as above) and Bruchollerie
(Gramophone ⊙ DA1888 – nla). Op. 135, con-
sisting of six *Etudes* for the left hand only, is of
interest primarily as an early but not overly

imaginative example of such studies, and the
outstanding recordings have been by Fleisher
(Sony Classical Ⓒ SK48081, 10/93) and Béroff
(EMI Ⓒ CDC7 49079-2, 9/89 – nla).

Piers Lane is thus in competition with some of
the greatest pianists of the century. In the 'Etude
en forme de valse' he sounds merely fast and
charmless, approaching neither Cortot's magically light double notes in the final pages nor the
suave *leggiero* qualities of Tagliaferro and
Duchâble throughout. But in the 'Toccata' his
brilliant and assured pianism matches the best
recordings I know. Elsewhere he provides intelligent, alert and sometimes colourful readings
that make this complete set preferable to the
relatively routine ones by Ringeissen (Adès ⊙
7069) and Dosse (Vox ⊙ SVBX5476 – nla) – but
not to the extraordinary one by Duchâble.
Hyperion's sound is always lovely, but I sometimes wished for less warmth in the bass and
more brilliance in the treble, especially in the
more demonstrative works. Lane's inclusion of
the challenging *Thème varié* provides a welcome
major work, played with real conviction, and his
informative booklet-notes add to this disc's
desirability. **Charles Timbrell**

Sauer Etudes de concert Nos. 21–30. Boîte à
Musique. Couplet sans Paroles. Les Délices
de Vienne. Echo de Vienne. Le Retour.
Scherzo Valse. **Oleg Marshev** (pf).
Danacord Ⓟ Ⓒ DACOCD488 (72 minutes:
DDD).

Hard on the heels of Vol. 1 (Ⓒ DACOCD487,
W/99) comes the second disc of Marshev's enter-
prising survey of the piano music of Emil von
Sauer, containing the remaining *Etudes de concert* and a selection of waltzes for good measure.
More so than in the first volume, the studies on
this disc tend towards a finger-crunching toccata style (whether Mendelssohnian or Ravelian
in character) rather than Chopinesque poetry,
although there are notable exceptions (No. 26,
'Preghiera', for example, or the extended No. 28,
'Waldandacht', for the left hand alone). The
nostalgic Viennese charm of the earlier waltzes
offers a happy and delicious contrast, evoking a
bygone era much as Godowsky and Ignaz
Friedman were later to do.

The apparent ease with which Oleg Marshev
encompasses such a range of demanding piano

writing is impressive, especially when, as here, there is no significant performance tradition to speak of, and therefore limited inherited parameters of interpretation. True, these works don't require deep insights or a special spiritual affinity; they do, however, require tremendous clarity and dexterity and an insouciant grace and charm, and in this Marshev is largely successful. He tackles works such as the 'Etude chromatique' (No. 21) and the 'Toccata' (No. 23) with untroubled fluency and aplomb, 'Le vertige' (No. 22) shimmers with menacing agitation, and the 'Staccato-Etude' (No. 29) reveals wrists of steel.

In some of the more lyrical pieces, however, I miss the delicacy and tonal beauty found on Sauer's own recordings. In 'Preghiera' for example, after a beautifully moulded *pianissimo* opening, Marshev's tone hardens palpably at louder dynamics; something of Sauer's fragrant sound world and sensuous tonal palette – or, if you like, a stronger erotic charge – would be more seductive. In the waltzes, too, Marshev's playing is most attractive at softer dynamic levels. But this is not a major quibble; if anything, this disc is more varied and attractive than its predecessor. Indeed, try Marshev's delightfully evocative music box (track 15) and you'll hear exquisitely graded and superbly crystalline passagework, surely accompanying the most elegant and pristine ballerina.

The recordings are quite close, which may accentuate the hardness of tone at *forte* level, and Farhan Malik's accompanying notes are illuminating and supply a broader context for the music. Volume 3 of this enjoyable survey, containing Sauer's two piano sonatas, should follow soon, and given the success of the first two discs I am looking forward to it impatiently.

Tim Parry

Great Pianists of the 20th Century – Jorge Bolet Jorge Bolet (pf).

Philips Great Pianists of the 20th Century Ⓜ Ⓒ 456 724-2PM2 (146 minutes: ADD). Items marked [a] from RCA ARL2-0512 and recorded at a performance in Carnegie Hall, New York on February 25th, 1974, [b] ARL1-0357 (recorded 1973), [c] Pye Ensayo NEL21013 (6/74).
Released in association with Steinway & Sons.

Bach/Rachmaninov: Solo Violin Partita No. 3 in E, BWV1006 – Prelude[b].
Bach/Busoni: Chaconne in D minor[a].
Bizet/Rachmaninov: L'Arlésienne – Menuet[b]. **Chopin:** 24 Preludes, Op. 28[a].
Donizetti/Liszt: Réminiscences de Lucia di Lammermoor, S397[c]. **Kreisler/Rachmaninov:** Liebesleid[b]. Liebesfreud[b].
Mendelssohn/Rachmaninov: A Midsummer Night's Dream – Scherzo[b].
Moszkowski: La jongleuse, Op. 52 No. 4[a].
Mussorgsky/Rachmaninov: Gopak[b].
Rachmaninov: Polka de W. R.[b].
Rimsky-Korsakov/Rachmaninov: The tale of Tsar Saltan – Flight of the bumble-bee[a].
Rubinstein: Study in C, 'Staccato', Op. 23[a].
J. Strauss II/Schulz-Evler: An die schönen Blauen Donau[a]. **J. Strauss II/Tausig:** Nouvelles soirées de Vienne[a] – Nachtfalter, Op. 157; Man lebt nur einmal, Op. 167.
Tchaikovsky/Rachmaninov: Cradle song, Op. 16 No. 1[b]. **Wagner/Liszt:** Tannhäuser Overture, S442[a].

There is general agreement among those familiar with Bolet's fabled Carnegie Hall performance from a quarter of a century ago that it ranks among the most inspired solo piano recitals ever captured on disc. Originally issued on two LPs, the programme has more recently been accessible only in truncated form on a single RCA CD (Ⓒ 7710-2-RG – never released in Britain) containing just the Chopin, Bach/Busoni and Wagner/Liszt items. Philips therefore deserves commendation for making the entire recital once again available, coupling it with a first CD release of Bolet's superb Rachmaninov transcription album (an RCA studio recording from 1973). Incidentally, this is the first of two Bolet releases within the Philips series; Vol. 2 will be entirely devoted to Liszt, drawn from the pianist's later Decca/London sessions.

A daunting programme that would be a trial by fire or an endurance test for nearly any other pianist becomes a regal feast for Bolet, a celebration of the magnificence of the piano as an instrument when the performer, repertoire, audience and auditorium all meld into a unique, extraordinary occasion. Bolet's magisterial approach to the Bach/Busoni *Chaconne* creates a towering edifice replete with a wealth of sophisticated pianistic detail. His journey through the Chopin *Preludes* focuses on the cycle's contrasts of mood, each piece sharply characterized with a degree of tonal and rhythmic subtlety beyond the reach of most other virtuosos. Once the second half is underway, however, it becomes apparent that Bolet is just beginning to get into his stride. His daring programming of not one, not two, but three Strauss waltz paraphrases, each selected for its individual qualities, is fully justified by the intoxicating, iridescent pianism that he lavishes on the music. Following the best traditions of his 'golden age' predecessors, Bolet makes a number of small textual adjustments throughout all three waltzes, thus enhancing the scores with added harmonic or pianistic spice (but always in the best of taste). Then, summoning forth all his considerable resources, Bolet offers the *Tannhäuser* Overture in a performance that makes most orchestral renditions of the work seem insignificant. The Carnegie Hall audience cheers him to the skies, and the Moszkowski and Rubinstein encores provide the perfect ending.

By contrast, a slight excess of sobriety, not so evident in the live recital, permeates Bolet's studio recording of the Rachmaninov transcriptions. Still, the level of pianism we encounter here is remarkable by any standard and it is a pleasure to welcome this collection back into the catalogue. One wonders why Bolet elected not to include the two additional movements of the Bach/Rachmaninov E major *Partita* (or for that matter, Rachmaninov's transcription of Schubert's *Wohin?*), but this is a minor point. The Liszt paraphrase on the *Lucia* sextet is Bolet's recording from *c*1970 that was first released by Ensayo, later by RCA, although the Philips credits claim ignorance of its origins. The performance finds Bolet on superb form.

Sonically these discs capture the sonority and dynamic range of Bolet's Baldwin instrument in the Carnegie Hall acoustic with reasonable accuracy, but the CD mastering from Philips seems curiously deficient in the bass end – a factor less evident on the original LP pressings. Much of the needed richness and weight can be restored via a healthy low-end boost from a good pre-amp or equalizer.

In sum, this is a mandatory acquisition and one of the highlights of this massive but wildly uneven project.   **Donald Manildi**

Great Pianists of the 20th Century – Shura Cherkassky Shura Cherkassky (pf).

Philips Great Pianists of the 20th Century mono/[ef]stereo Ⓜ ① 456 742-2PM2 (two discs: 160 minutes: ADD). Item marked [a] from HMV ALP1310/11 (2/56), [b]HMV DB9599-600 (4/53), [c]DB21137 (4/53), [d]World Record Club T247 (recorded 1963), [e]ASV CDQS6109 (1968), [f]Decca 433 650-2DH (6/93). Released in association with Steinway & Sons.

Chopin: Etudes – Op. 10; Op. 25; Op. posth[a]. Fantasie in F minor, Op. 49[b]. Mazurka No. 23 in D, Op. 33 No. 2[c]. Barcarolle in F sharp, Op. 60[d]. Nocturne No. 15 in F minor, Op. 55 No. 1[d]. Preludes, Op. 28[e]. Piano Sonata No. 3 in B minor, Op. 58[f].

The surge of interest during the Indian Summer of Shura Cherkassky's career was complemented and furthered by the series of eight CDs from Decca produced by the late Peter Wadland. These performances originated from BBC broadcasts of live concerts, a medium where Cherkassky is heard at his best; indeed, I remember him saying to me on one occasion that he didn't feel he came over well on record and although this, in part, was true (due to his need of an audience), much of his studio work is of a very high quality.

During the early 1950s Cherkassky made a considerable number of recordings for EMI, some of which have appeared on a Testament disc, mainly of works by Liszt (① SBT1033, 9/94). Some of his Chopin recordings from this same period are presented here on CD for the first time.

The *Etudes* were recorded between 1953 and 1955 but the difference in sound quality between the tracks does not detract from the enjoyment of the performances. There are recordings of these pieces where pianists just play the notes as fast as possible and lose sight of the music, but when listening to Cherkassky one has a totally musical experience that is perhaps unexpectedly close to the text in many respects. How nice it is to hear the *diminuendo* at the end of Op. 10 No. 1, and the two-bar *stretto* of Op. 10 No. 6 lasting for its marked two bars, the pervading melancholy mood being perfectly captured with a beautiful singing line. Being Cherkassky, he does, of course, do unexpected things: a *pianissimo* ending to Op. 10 No. 8 *à la* Horowitz; Op. 10 No. 9 is not at all *molto agitato*, and he seems to hurry through the rests and pauses in Op. 25 No. 7. No matter; the sweep of the final three *Etudes* from Op. 25 makes up for any minor quibbles. No. 10 has an unbridled ferocity whilst the melody of No. 12 tolls like a bell through a torrent of arpeggios.

The *Mazurka*, Op. 33 No. 2 and the *Fantasie* are those from 1950 (by which time EMI were using tape), first issued on 78s. The piano tone is noticeably harder in the *Mazurka*, but still good considering the recording is practically 50 years old!

The *Barcarolle* and the F minor *Nocturne* were first issued in 1963; the *Barcarolle* shows Cherkassky at his very best, all the hallmarks are there – the glorious warm tone, beautiful *legato*, delicate *pianissimos* and ecstatic climaxes. It reminded me of another recording of his on the Tudor label (⊙ 720) which he made in October 1976. This elusive disc also contains amongst other Chopin works the F minor *Fantasie* and the First and Second *Ballades*. However, a glance at the timings of the *Barcarolle* shows that the Tudor performance takes 7'43" whilst this earlier EMI recording lasts an expansive 9'10". Cherkassky's secret of retaining the rapt attention of the audience (and himself!) in music that is so familiar is one of his greatest attributes. Initially, I was disappointed to see the familiar F minor *Nocturne* programmed rather than the rarely heard E major *Waltz*, Op. posth. (which was also on the original LP), but the performance of the *Nocturne* is so hypnotic that my disappointment quickly evaporated.

Although Cherkassky recorded the Chopin *Preludes* in 1968, they were not issued until 1995, on ASV. Both these and the superlative B minor Sonata from a Royal Festival Hall performance are still currently available, as is a live performance of the *Preludes* from the Salzburg Festival in 1968 (Orfeo ① C4319621). It is almost impossible to represent Cherkassky's art on four CDs (a second instalment is to follow, containing *concertante* works) but Chopin is the obvious first choice.

Any reissues of Cherkassky are welcome, this one in particular for the *Etudes* and *Barcarolle*. It is hoped that we will see further releases of his discs from the 1950s such as the famous recording of Prokofiev's Second Piano Concerto (coupled with Shostakovich's First), the Third

Sonata of Hindemith or anything else from the four or five LPs (including Beethoven's Op. 111 and the Grieg and Schumann Concertos with Boult and the LSO) made for the World Record Club in the early 1960s, all of which captured Cherkassky's unique marvellous sound.

Jonathan Summers

....

Great Pianists of the 20th Century – Lyubov Bruk and Mark Taimanov

Lyubov Bruk, Mark Taimanov (pfs); [a]**Leningrad Chamber Orchestra / Lazar Gozman;** [b]**Leningrad Philharmonic Orchestra / Arnold Katz.**
Philips Great Pianists of the 20th Century mono/[c]stereo Ⓜ ① 456 736-2PM2 (two discs: 156 minutes: ADD). Released in association with Steinway & Sons.
Arensky: Suites – No. 1 in F, Op. 15 (Melodiya D015391/2. Recorded 1964); No. 2, 'Silhouettes', Op. 23 (D04994/5. 1959). **Busoni:** Duettino concertante nach dem Finale von Mozarts Klavierkonzert, K459 (D015391/2. 1964). **Chopin:** Rondo in C, Op. 73 (D04994/5. 1959). **Milhaud:** Scaramouche, Op. 165*b* (D027221/2. 1968). **Mozart:** Concerto for Two Pianos and Orchestra in E flat, K365/K316*a* (S01275/6. 1966)[ac]. **Poulenc:** Concerto for Two Pianos and Orchestra in D minor (S0793/4. 1963)[bc]. Sonata for Two Pianos (SM02271/2. 1962)[c]. **Rachmaninov:** Suites – No. 1, 'Fantaisie-tableaux', Op. 5 (D04994/5. 1959); No. 2, Op. 17 (SM02271/2. 1962)[c].

Of all the Russian artists included in Philips's series, the husband-and-wife two-piano team of Lyubov Bruk and Mark Taimanov may be the least familiar names to Western listeners. According to the excellent annotation, the duo had only just begun touring outside the Soviet bloc when both their on- and off-stage partnerships dissolved in the early 1970s. This generous selection from their Melodiya recordings, however, attests to the duo's uncanny synchronicity of fingers and spirit. Unanimity of chordal attacks, for instance, reveals not one tell-tale 'kerplonk', while their liquid yet pinpointed phrasing and delicate tempo fluctuations, if I may risk a cliché, sound as if they were coming from one mega-piano, with a single master operating keys and pedals.

With the exception of the Mozart E flat Concerto for two pianos, the repertoire, though not insubstantial, is essentially confectionary in nature, and best savoured one or two works at a time. If Moszkowski wrote the best salon music for piano four-hands, Anton Arensky's Suites take top honours in the two-piano medium. The outer movements of the First Suite are in no way inferior to the famous middle movement 'Waltz', tossed off with quicksilver lilt and an unwritten, yet surprisingly effective *accelerando* in the concluding bars. Similarly, Arensky's Second Suite and Chopin's early, underrated C major *Rondo* sing with with effortless interplay and transparent balances, as does Milhaud's samba-tinged *Scaramouche.* Perhaps the latter's finale is a shade too fast for comfort (more 'Troika' than 'Tico-Tico'!), but the duo's winged rendition of Busoni's *Duettino concertante* manages to make this perverse recasting of the finale of Mozart's F major Concerto, K459 palatable. It would be hard to find more flexible and idiomatic versions of the two Rachmaninov Suites, and I am not forgetting cherished recordings by the likes of Vronsky and Babin (Dante ① HPC026), Ginzburg/Goldenweiser (Melodiya ① 74321 25173-2, 8/95), and Argerich/Freire (Philips ① 411 034-2PH, 2/84). But the cavernous, petrol-tank acoustic in Suite No. 2 is as hard on the ears as the steel-coated miking that mars the otherwise excellent Poulenc selections, to say nothing of the ill-tuned pianos in the latter's concerto. While the aforementioned Mozart concerto is more tolerable from an engineering vantage point, the stilted orchestral execution is akin to one wearing a brown tweed suit to the beach. The pianists treat Mozart with kid gloves, making beautifully tapered phrases that only hint at the drama and sinew beneath the notes.

Piano ensemble connoisseurs will find a treasure trove here, but less specialized listeners may have trouble getting past the sonic inconsistencies. Sample, if you can, before buying.

Jed Distler

EMI French Pianists
Marguerite Long Marguerite Long (pf); Paris Conservatoire Orchestra / [ab]André Cluytens, [c]Georges Tzipine, [f]Charles Munch; [e]Paris Symphony Orchestra / Philippe Gaubert; [d]orchestra / Darius Milhaud.

EMI French Pianists mono ⑧ ① CZS5 72245-2 (two discs: 141 minutes: ADD). Item marked [a] from French Columbia FCX193 (recorded 1953), [b]Columbia LX8953/4 (2/53), [c]FCX169 (1952), [d]French Columbia LFX375/6 (1935), [e]LX527/9 (10/36), [f]LFX679/83 (1944).
Chopin: Concerto for Piano and Orchestra No. 2 in F minor, Op. 21[a]. **Fauré:** Ballade in F sharp, Op. 19[b]. **Ravel:** Concerto for Piano and Orchestra in G[c]. **Milhaud:** Concerto for Piano and Orchestra No. 1, Op. 127[d].
Mozart: Concerto for Piano and Orchestra No. 23 in A, K488[e]. **Beethoven:** Concerto for Piano and Orchestra No. 5 in E flat, 'Emperor', Op. 73[f].

In recent years EMI has been very generous in reissuing recordings by historic French pianists. First came large helpings of Alfred Cortot, Marcelle Meyer and Samson François, then the 1997 release of two-disc sets devoted to Jeanne-Marie Darré, Yves Nat, Jacques Février, Yvonne Lefébure, Magda Tagliaferro and Robert and Jean Casadesus (reviewed A/97). The present four sets round out the picture with discs featuring Marguerite Long and her Italian protégé Aldo Ciccolini, as well as the remastering of items from the extensive discographies of Cortot and François.

Marguerite Long (1874-1966) was the grandest of the French 'grandes dames'. She was coached by Debussy and became the friend and champion of d'Indy, Fauré, Ravel, Milhaud and dozens of other French composers. Her influence was enormous, especially as a teacher (among her successful students were Février, François, Darré, Gaby Casadesus and Entremont). After teaching for nearly 35 years at the Conservatoire, she founded her own school and taught international master-classes in Paris. Despite her gift for self-promotion (her book about her few days of study with Debussy is a prime example), she was an inspiring figure for numerous artists. Her technique, which epitomized the old French school, was almost completely digital, with little use of the arm, shoulder or foot. It worked for much French music, for Mozart and for certain works by Chopin – but certainly not very well for Beethoven, Liszt, Brahms or Rachmaninov.

The Chopin and Ravel concertos heard here are unfortunately inferior to her earlier versions (a 1929 account of the Chopin, conducted by Philippe Gaubert, and a 1932 version of the Ravel, conducted – not by Ravel, as originally advertised – but by Pedro de Freitas-Branco, EMI ⓓ CDH5 65499-2, 12/96). Certainly there are some impressive things in her 1952 Chopin recording, but at this point in her career her playing often sounded disengaged. Her account is also marred by frequent rhythmic distortions, a tendency to 'prettify' the music (as after 4'42" in the first movement) and a surprisingly mechanical approach to the expressive *gruppetti* (as after 9'15" in the first movement and in much of the slow movement). She even blatantly changes Chopin's right-hand scale in thirds (at 8'35" in the first movement) to a scale in single notes. Although Long played and taught this concerto often, neither of her recordings comes close to attaining the natural elegance and nobility of Cortot's account (1935, conducted by Sir John Barbirolli, EMI ⓓ CZS7 67359-2, 6/92 – nla).

The Ravel G major Concerto was long identified with Long, from its première in 1932 (with Ravel conducting) to her final performances of it in the 1950s. In this 1952 account the first two movements are noticeably slower than in her 1932 version (for which the orchestra had been rehearsed by Ravel beforehand). Furthermore, the *meno vivo* sections of the first movement are disappointingly brusque and the cadenza quite choppy. Only the finale matches the earlier recording's lively elegance. Of course, the recorded sound is much clearer here, although the remastering gives it a close and rather hard edge – as is also true of the Chopin.

Fauré's *Ballade* was Long's war-horse for four decades, and this 1952 account is far less sectional and self-consciously flashy than her 1931 version (conducted by Gaubert; reviewed W/97). In fact, it may be the most poised of all her Fauré recordings. (In her accounts of Fauré's solo works she often sounds restless and unfocused, as though overly conscious of needing to fit the music on to one or two sides of a 78.) It is also good to have the brief, neo-classical and often sassy Milhaud Concerto back in the catalogue, recorded by composer and dedicatee a few months after its première. The Mozart and Beethoven concertos, recorded in 1939 and 1944 respectively, provide interesting documentation of French pianistic and orchestral approaches to the Viennese classical repertory. The Mozart is

full of wit and verve, with a particularly touching slow movement and excellent solo playing from the winds. In the Beethoven, however, Long is miscast, and her playing – clean almost to a fault – lacks the requisite breadth and grandeur. In short, the set is recommendable mostly for the Fauré, Milhaud and Mozart, and all three are carefully remastered. In the effusive essay that accompanies the set, André Tubeuf distorts the facts in at least one instance in an effort to make a colourful story about Long sound even more so. And so myths grow and grow.

Charles Timbrell

EMI French Pianists

Alfred Cortot Alfred Cortot (pf).
EMI French Pianists mono ⓑ ⓓ CZS5 72248-2 (two discs: 121 minutes: ADD).
Items marked [a] from HMV DB6725/6 (recorded 1947), [b]HMV DA1240/4 (6/32), [c]DB6726 (1947), [d]DB9578 (2/51), [e]DB1533/4 (6/32), [f]DB643 (1923), [g]DB1307/9 (5/30), [h]DB1042 (10/27), [i]DA952 (2/31), [j]DB1105 (12/28), [k]DB3269 (1/40), [l]DB1535 (6/32).
Debussy: Children's Corner[a]. Préludes, Book 1 – Danseuses de Delphes[b]; Voiles[b]; Le vent dans la plaine[b]; Les sons et les parfums[b]; Les collines d'Anacapri[b]; Des pas sur la neige[b]; Ce qu'a vu le vent d'Ouest[b]; La fille aux cheveux de lin[b]; La sérénade interrompué[b]; La cathédrale engloutie[c]; La danse de Puck[d]; Minstrels[b]. **Ravel:** Piano Sonatine[e]. Jeux d'eau[f]. **Liszt:** Piano Sonata in B minor, S178[g]. Hungarian Rhapsodies, S244 – No. 2 in C sharp minor[h]; No. 11 in A minor[i]. Rigoletto Paraphrase, S434[j]. St Francis de Paule walking on the water, S175 No. 2[k]. La leggierezza, S144 No. 2[l].

How very unfortunate that EMI has decided to reissue some of Cortot's least satisfactory recordings of Debussy. Instead of providing the complete 1930/1 account of the First Book of *Préludes*, they have given a producer's composite version that inexplicably includes inferior performances of 'La cathédrale engloutie', from 1947, and 'La danse de Puck', from 1949. This circumstance is alluded to in the accompanying essay by Alain Cochard and is only apparent from checking the fine print about the provenance of each *Prélude* – though even there the information given is incorrect. The entire set of *Préludes* is compromised by very poor transfers. And instead of the superior 1928 recording of *Children's Corner* we are given a lumpy and brusque version from 1947. These performances, and the way they have been remastered, give only a hint of the miraculous colourism, alert humour and wonderful variety of touch that Cortot could bring to Debussy's music, I urge the reader to acquire the superior versions issued together on Biddulph (℗ LHW006, 6/92, with excellent remastering and full documentation).

Cortot's greatness is abundantly clear in his famous recording of Liszt's Sonata, a blazing account that has held up very well for almost 70 years. Occasional technical imperfections count for nothing, so grand is the conception and so intense the poetry. The section from 11'00" to 16'00" is memorable for the way it moves steadily and inevitably from the most noble simplicity to the most feverish rhetoric – just as the passages from 19'00" to the end move in the opposite musical direction. The *Rigoletto* Paraphrase and Second *Hungarian Rhapsody*, also from the late 1920s, are equally riveting in their virtuosity and colourism, while *La leggierezza* is a model of stylish filigree playing. The remastering, however, is poor and I recommend that the serious collector of Cortot's Liszt acquires these works on Pearl ℗ GEMMCD9396. **Charles Timbrell**

....

EMI French Pianists
Aldo Ciccolini Aldo Ciccolini (pf).
EMI French Pianists mono Ⓑ ℗ CZS5 72251-2 (two discs: 150 minutes: ADD).
Items marked ᵃ from French Columbia ESBF104, ᵇFrench Columbia FC1028, ᶜᵈᵉFrench Columbia FCX613, ᶠFrench Columbia FCX441, ᵍʰFr Columbia FCX651, ⁱʲᵏˡFrench Columbia FCX652.

D. Scarlatti: Keyboard Sonatasᵃ – D minor, Kk64; G, Kk259; A, Kk268; D minor, Kk459. **Mozart:** Piano Sonata No. 11 in A, K331/K300*i*ᵇ. **Liszt:** Six Consolations, S172ᶜ. Ballade No. 2 in B minor, S171ᵈ. Mephisto Waltz No. 1, S514ᵉ. Années de pèlerinage – Deuxième année: Italie, S161ᶠ – Sonetto 123 del Petrarca. **Albéniz:** España, Op. 165ᵍ. **Mompou:** Cançons i dansasʰ – Nos. 1-8. **Borodin:** Petite Suiteⁱ. **Arensky:** Scherzo in A, Op. 8ʲ. **Kabalevsky:** Piano Sonatina No. 1 in C, Op. 13 No. 1ᵏ. **Stravinsky:** Tangoˡ.

It may seem odd that Aldo Ciccolini is included in EMI's series of French pianists, as he couldn't be more Italian. He was born in 1925 in Naples and received his musical education at that city's Conservatory, where he studied the piano with Paolo Denza, a pupil of Busoni. But after winning First Prize in the 1949 Marguerite Long Competition he moved to France, had some coaching from Long, Cortot and Nat, became a naturalized French citizen in 1969, and was appointed professor at the Paris Conservatoire from 1971 to 1989.

Although he remains active as a performer today, the recordings on this set all date from the 1950s and hence almost qualify for 'historical' status. The first disc seems to have been planned as a recital programme, ranging as it does from some sparkling Scarlatti sonatas (incorrectly identified on the package) to an oddly winning performance of Mozart's K331 (despite its inconsistent observance of dynamic marks and repeat signs, and the strange omission of ten bars in the sixth variation) and a generous but uneven Liszt group. It is not Ciccolini's fault that the six *Consolations* have a soporific effect when played as a group; but he must take the blame for making such dramatic works as the B minor *Ballade* and *Mephisto Waltz* sound so musically uneventful. He sails through the most difficult passages with total aplomb, with octaves as fast as lightning and arpeggios and repeated notes that are so clear and uniform that one could take dictation from them. The important missing element is Cortot's brand of musical involvement – of realizing the notes with sweep and passion, in sentences and paragraphs rather than in clauses and phrases. The dreamy 'Sonetto 123 del Petrarca' finds Ciccolini more in his element, coaxing beautiful sounds from the instrument.

Although he regularly performs the middle and late sonatas of Beethoven and Schubert, I have always found Ciccolini to be most successful in miniatures – starting with his first recordings of Satie. So it is not surprising to find him completely at home in the short pieces by Spanish and Russian composers that make up the second disc. The Albéniz set is full of tight rhythms and loose innuendoes, all realized with easy virtuosity and subtle colouring. The Mompou pieces are played with disarming charm and unforced characterization (and they compare well with the recent versions by

Stephen Hough – Hyperion ℗ CDA66963, Au/97). The Arensky and Borodin are of less inherent interest (except for the latter's 'Au couvent' from the *Petite Suite*), the Kabalevsky is raised from its usual status as a teaching piece to a virtuosic delight, and the Stravinsky *Tango* could hardly be played with more infectious sultriness. Despite some reservations, this set – like all but Cortot's in this series – is definitely worth acquiring, and even more so at bargain price. **Charles Timbrell**

....

EMI French Pianists
Chopin Piano Works. **Samson François** (pf). EMI French Pianists mono ℗ ℗ CZS5 72242-2 (two discs: 154 minutes: ADD). Andante spianato and Grande Polonaise in E flat, Op. 22 – Grande polonaise. Ballades – No. 1 in G minor, Op. 23; No. 4 in F minor, Op. 52. Barcarolle in F sharp, Op. 60. Etudes – Op. 10: No. 3 in E; No. 5 in G flat; No. 10 in A flat; No. 12 in C minor; Op. 25: No. 2 in F minor; No. 5 in E minor. Fantaisie-impromptu in C sharp minor, Op. 66. Fantasie in F minor, Op. 49. Impromptu No. 1 in A flat, Op. 29. Nocturnes – No. 2 in E flat, Op. 9 No. 2; No. 4 in F, Op. 15 No. 1; No. 5 in F sharp, Op. 15 No. 2. Piano Sonata No. 2 in B flat minor, 'Funeral March', Op. 35. Polonaise No. 6 in A flat, 'Heroic', Op. 53. Prelude No. 1 in C, Op. 28. Scherzos – No. 2 in B flat minor, Op. 31; No. 3 in C sharp minor, Op. 39. Tarantelle in A flat, Op. 43. Waltzes – No. 1 in E flat, Op. 18; No. 6 in D flat, Op. 64 No. 1; No. 7 in C sharp minor, Op. 64 No. 2; No. 9 in A flat, Op. 69 No. 1; No. 11 in G flat, Op. 70 No. 1; No. 13 in D flat, Op. 70 No. 3.

Samson François (1924-70) studied at the Ecole Normale with Cortot and Lefébure, performed Liszt's *Réminiscences de Don Juan* at the age of 14, and received a first prize at the Conservatoire in Long's class in 1940. While his big-scaled, free interpretations owed much to Cortot's example, it is certain that his unruly personality received much-needed discipline from Long. In fact, Long claimed that François was the only student that she ever slapped. Her efforts, however, did not make him a less wilful musician. His numerous recordings –

which include most of the works of Chopin, Debussy and Ravel as well as major helpings of Liszt, Prokofiev and Schumann – are quite uneven. Although he was capable of mesmerizing concert audiences when he was on good form, the force of his hypnotic personality does not come through on recordings. Instead, his liberties with the text, sometimes to the point of recomposing the notes, can be quite irksome. In France in the early 1960s, however, his instinctive musicianship and personal iconoclasm were admired because he stood out against the more intellectual performance trends and had something personal and immediate to communicate. Today there seems to be a justified revival of interest in his recordings.

On the present discs there are several works that might well qualify him for consideration as one of the major pianists of the century. Certainly his 1955 recording of Op. 22 (without the *Andante spianato*) is one of the most stylish, polished and elegant versions on record. And for sheer speed and clarity, not even Horowitz surpassed his accounts of Op. 53, Op. 10 No. 5 or the hair-raising final four minutes of Op. 23. On a purely musical plane, I especially admire the breadth and virility of his conception of Op. 31 (which he clearly did not regard as the 'Governess' *Scherzo*!), the wonderful lightness and shimmer of Op. 29, and the straightforward but affecting musicianship evident in Op. 15 No. 2.

These examples of virtuosity, taste and refinement are unfortunately counterbalanced by an equal number of disappointments: punchy, unsteady playing in Op. 35 and Op. 60; outrageous rhythmic and melodic distortions in Op. 10 No. 12; a rewriting of Op. 28 No. 1 and the left-hand part of the slow movement of Op. 35; wilful altering of dynamics and articulations in many of the waltzes; and numerous octave doublings added in virtually every work. But even in the extremely erratic and sloppy Op. 39 there are occasional moments of ravishing pianism.

The remastering is quite natural-sounding, and the choice and sequence of pieces has been determined with some care. However, I would have preferred a different sampling from the 24 *Etudes* and would have welcomed the inclusion of at least one of the 51 *Mazurkas* that François recorded at his height in 1956.

Charles Timbrell

Ignaz Friedman – Highlights from his Discography Ignaz Friedman (pf).

APR Signature mono Ⓜ Ⓓ APR5508 (77 minutes: ADD). **Beethoven:** Piano Sonata No. 14 in C sharp minor, 'Moonlight', Op. 27 No. 2 (from Columbia L1818/9, 2/27). **Chopin:** Etudes – C, Op. 10 No. 7; C minor, 'Revolutionary', Op. 10 No. 12 (both from American Columbia 7119M, recorded 1926). Polonaise No. 6 in A flat, 'Heroic', Op. 53 (L1990, 10/27). Piano Sonata No. 2 in B flat minor, 'Funeral March', Op. 35 – Marche funèbre; Presto (Australian Columbia 04007. 1927). Etudes – G flat, Op. 10 No. 5; G flat, Op. 25 No. 9 (both from Columbia D1615, 9/28). Mazurkas – No. 17 in B flat minor, Op. 24 No. 4; No. 25 in B minor, Op. 33 No. 4 (both previously unpublished. Recorded 1929 or 1930). Impromptu No. 2 in F sharp, Op. 36. Nocturne No. 16 in E flat, Op. 55 No. 2 (both Columbia DX781, 8/37). Waltz No. 9 in A flat, Op. 69 No. 1 (previously unpublished. 1929). **Friedman:** Elle danse, Op. 10 No. 5 (Columbia D1558, 2/27). Music Box, Op. 33 No. 3 (D1651, 5/29). **Hummel:** Rondo in E flat, Op. 11, 'Rondo favori' (Columbia L1750). **Liszt:** La campanella, S141 No. 3 (arr. Busoni and Friedman. L1804, 1/27). Ständchen von Shakespeare, 'Horch, horch, die Lerch', S558 (Columbia D1636, 2/29). **Mendelssohn:** Scherzo in E minor, Op. 16 No. 2 (D1558). **Shield** (arr. Friedman): Old English Minuet (previously unpublished. 1929).

Since 1990, collectors of Friedman's unique pianism have been reasonably well served by the four-disc Pearl set (Ⓓ IF2000, 12/90) containing all his then-known recordings except the Beethoven *Kreutzer* Sonata with Huberman (which was reissued by EMI Références on Ⓓ CDH7 63194-2, 2/90). Prior to the Pearl collection, a pioneering Danacord LP offered different transfers of the pianist's complete legacy. Additional CDs of various Friedman items, brought out by assorted French and Italian entrepreneurs, would seem to have 'borrowed' their source material from the earlier releases.

Now we have fresh transfers from APR of 18 selected sides, augmented by the first release of a pair of Chopin *Mazurkas* in alternate takes, and two more items new to the Friedman

discography. The latter, of course, carry the most interest. The Chopin A flat *Waltz* – an elegantly conceived, highly nuanced interpretation with some unexpected textual alterations – is of such quality that minor sonic deficiencies are of little moment. To be specific, the slightly fuzzy quality of the surviving test pressing sometimes obliterates left-hand detail, and the transfer here is nearly a semitone sharp. The same problems appear in the *Old English Minuet*, but again Friedman's playing contains such colour and style that any such quibbles are insignificant. As for the two *Mazurkas*, they perhaps contain less finely-judged detail and coherence when compared to Friedman's later approved versions, yet every existing recording by a pianist of his calibre offers invaluable pianistic information.

The other works require little comment at this late date. The overall selection gives a representative sampling from Friedman's recordings, with the four Chopin *Etudes* and the E flat *Nocturne* in particular containing playing on a consummate level of imagination and individuality. The transfers of these pieces are skilfully done, and they capture Friedman's tonal qualities to an admirable extent. **Donald Manildi**

Great Pianists of the 20th Century – Leon Fleisher Leon Fleisher (pf);

[d]Cleveland Orchestra / George Szell; [f]Baltimore Symphony Orchestra / Sergiu Comissiona.

Philips Great Pianists of the 20th Century mono/stereo Ⓜ Ⓓ 456 775-2PM2 (two discs: 159 minutes: ADD/DDD). Items marked [a] from Epic BC1262 (recorded 1963), [b]Epic LC3675 (1959), [c]LC3584 (1958), [d]LC3330 (1956), [e]LC3554 (1958), [f]Vanguard VSD25014 (1982). Released in association with Steinway & Sons.
Copland: Piano Sonata[a]. **Liszt:** Piano Sonata in B minor, S178[b]. **Mozart:** Piano Sonata No. 10 in C, K330/K300*h*[c]. **Rachmaninov:** Rhapsody on a Theme of Paganini, Op. 43[d]. **Ravel:** Sonatine[e]. Alborada del gracioso[e]. Concerto for Piano (Left-Hand) and Orchestra in D[f]. **Rorem:** Three Barcarolles[a]. **Weber:** Piano Sonata No. 4 in E minor, J287[b].

Unlike some of the volumes in this Philips project, the Fleisher compilation has been assembled with a view toward restoring some of this pianist's choicest recordings to the catalogues. Indeed, all the solo items here, except for the Ravel 'Alborada', appear on CD for the first time.

Although he programmed very few of Liszt's works during the early phase of his career, Fleisher's compelling interpretation of the B minor Sonata reveals him to be a Liszt interpreter of rare quality. While avoiding rhetorical excess, and unfolding the musical events with unerring logic and taut control, Fleisher never allows the work to sag for a moment, sustaining impetus even in the most lyrical and contemplative sections. Where propulsion and intensity are called for, Fleisher supplies exactly what is needed. From a technical standpoint he is in complete command, and while other players may have displayed a wider coloristic palette in this work, Fleisher easily compensates through his intelligent integration of the score's diverse elements.

Much the same approach is applied to the Rachmaninov *Paganini* Rhapsody, and the obvious rapport between Fleisher and Szell makes for a true partnership of equals. (This, incidentally, was their first recorded collaboration, pre-dating their now famous, and still available, editions of the Beethoven, Brahms, Grieg and Schumann concertos.) Some may prefer a more lush, expansive and flexible treatment, but it is refreshing to be reminded of the lean modernity that is an important element of this 1934 masterpiece (an element that Rachmaninov himself emphasized in his own performances).

Fleisher offers an intense, idiomatic performance of the Copland Sonata that easily ranks alongside the superlative versions by Bernstein (RCA Victor Gold Seal ℗ GD60915), Kapell (RCA Victor Red Seal mono ℗ 09026 68442-2, A/98) and Leo Smit (Sony Classical ℗ SM2K66345, 6/81R – nla), while the attractive but rather lightweight Rorem *Barcarolles* provide an appropriate contrast. Those familiar with Fleisher's 1959 recording of the Mozart C major Concerto, K503 (Sony Classical ℗ CD44832 – nla) will find an interpretation of comparable distinction here in the K330 Sonata. Fleisher was undoubtedly influenced by his teacher Artur Schnabel's sense of Mozartian style, with its cultivation of a singing line, rhythmic vitality and keen projection of phraseology. Perhaps this Sonata's original disc-mate,

the E flat Sonata, K282, can be reissued in the near future.

Truly remarkable is the Weber Sonata, where exceptionally impressive pianism (notably in the Trio of the *Scherzo* and throughout the finale) is wedded to a no-nonsense conception of the score that brings out all its strengths and conceals its minor weaknesses. If the solo Ravel pieces are slightly lacking in the last degrees of colour and subtlety, the Left-Hand Concerto (heard here in the earlier of Fleisher's two recordings) has rarely been given a bigger, more dramatic treatment. From a sonic standpoint the remasterings have turned out well, and even the crisp, clean solo items in mono (Mozart, Weber, Liszt, Ravel) admirably capture the round yet incisive quality of Fleisher's tone.

Donald Manildi

The Complete Josef Hofmann, Volume 6.
Josef Hofmann (pf); orchestra / Sir John Barbirolli.
Marston mono ℗ ① 52014-2 (two discs: 149 minutes: ADD). Items marked [a] from IPL IPA5007/8 (3/70), [b]from a broadcast performance on March 15th, 1936, [c]October 26th, 1941, [d]from unpublished US Columbias (October 13th, 1916) 48946-4/5 and [e]July 31st, 1944.
Beethoven: Concerto for Piano and Orchestra No. 4 in G, Op. 58[c]. Piano Sonatas – No. 14 in C sharp minor, 'Moonlight', Op. 27 No. 2[b]; No. 14 in C sharp minor, 'Moonlight' Op. 27 No. 2 – Adagio sostenuto (three versions[de]); No. 21 in C, 'Waldstein', Op. 53[a]. **Chopin:** Ballade No. 4 in F minor, Op. 52[a]. Polonaise No. 2 in E flat minor, Op. 26 No. 2[a]. Nocturnes – No. 3 in B, Op. 9 No. 3[a]; No. 5 in F sharp, Op. 15 No. 2[b]. Waltzes – No. 1 in E-flat, Op. 18[a]; No. 5 in A flat, Op. 42[b]; No. 6 in D flat, 'Minute' Op. 64 No. 1 (arr. Hofmann)[a]; No. 6 in D flat, 'Minute' Op. 64 No. 1[b]. **Hofmann:** Three Impressions – No. 1, 'Penguine'[a]. Kaleidoskop, Op. 40 No. 4[a]. **Schubert/Godowsky:** Moment musical in F minor, D780 No. 3[a]. **Schumann:** Kreisleriana, Op. 16 (abridged)[a]. **Stojowski:** Caprice orientale, Op. 10 No. 2[a].

Edward Dent once observed that Busoni was not a pianist for beginners in the art of listening.

He had no interest in merely repeating ideas with which his audience was already thoroughly familiar, on the assumption that his listeners were as well acquainted with the classics as he was himself. The case of Josef Hofmann is in many respects not dissimilar, although the apoplexy created by some of his recorded legacy in certain quarters probably tells us more about the nature of post-war reception theory and the redefinition of interpretative criteria which it created than it does about any specific aspects of Hofmann's performance aesthetic.

As with Busoni, the extraordinary freedom exhibited in Hofmann's interpretations appears at times almost provocatively to fly in the face of convention. Yet, paradoxically, Hofmann's expressed view on textual fidelity, that a lifetime was insufficient to explore all the possibilities implicit in an accurate perception of the printed score, would suggest a stance more in keeping with a 'modernist' approach than with the reviled romantic egocentricity and capricious sensationalism of which he has often been accused. Where, for Busoni, the fusion of conflicting polarities may be described as 'passionate intellectuality', Hofmann's playing epitomizes a controlled impetuosity and a white-hot emotional intensity remarkable for its outward restraint, a restraint reflected in the self-composure of his stage demeanour and absence of histrionic mannerism.

Like Godowsky, Hofmann approached studio recording and public performance as two separate disciplines, sharing a common *modus operandi* yet with quite separate objectives. Interestingly, both of them undertook exhaustive technical reworking in preparation for studio sessions to accommodate shortcomings in the early recording process. Hofmann's fascination with the experimental and scientific aspects of sound recording *per se* must be weighed against his frustration at being limited by practical and commercial considerations to recording only encore-size pieces in the studio. It is, therefore, especially fortunate that several of his public performances of larger-scale repertoire should have survived, however perplexing they may appear to some more accustomed to the controlled sang-froid and, admittedly, occasionally almost prosaic disengagement of some of his studio output.

Arguably, the most controversial aspects of Hofmann's artistry are to be found in his interpretations of Beethoven, in which his apparent refusal to pursue the self-consciously reverential line has been variously judged as exploitation of the music solely for questionable pianistic effect and as a fundamental debasement of the most aristocratic principles of art. On the other hand, if Hofmann's performances were so misconceived and disregardful of the music's dignity and essential spirituality, then what is one to make of the extravagant endorsements of, for example, Stravinsky, Rachmaninov, Huneker and others, who considered Hofmann to be an interpretative genius? From this distance in time, we do, of course, draw conclusions based on post-Schnabelian criteria and for all the much-heralded modernity of Hofmann's approach at the time, nowadays his aesthetic appears more representative of a romantic performance tradition of which he was one of the last exponents. The perceived mutual exclusivity of emotion and scholarship, however, takes little account of the deeper traditions out of which each grew. The gaucherie which too readily mistakes sentiment for sentimentality and lack of imagination for interpretative objectivity has led to the type of all-pervasive aridity which has disfigured so much later playing.

Hofmann's protégé, the late Ezra Rachlin, unashamedly *parti pris*, proposes in a detailed analysis of the *Waldstein* performance which appears in the accompanying booklet a response indicating how the multiplicity of highly personal touches in Hofmann's reading, for all their contrariety, were, in fact, far from arbitrary and formed part of a logical, coherent exegesis of compelling authority.

Equally, Hofmann's cut version of *Kreisleriana* – he omits the third and fourth movements in their entirety and excises the second Intermezzo and the modulatory link which follows – pushes every aspect of the music to the outside limits of expressive intensity, the Florestan/Eusebius duality of the writing emerging with a vividness of contrast that defies definition. (In passing, before condemning out of hand Hofmann's 'surgery' on the work, it is worth noting Clara Schumann's comments to Brahms in 1858 that *Kreisleriana* 'seems so unsuitable for a concert ... it would never do to play them all'; even Lipatti found them 'much too long' in their entirety.) On the other hand, it could be said that tempos are so extreme in the fast movements as to allow no time for detail to be articulated and that dynamics are overprojected to the point of caricature. Yet his control of voicing, his differentiation and shaping of hidden counterpoints, the weighting and balance of part-writing, even in such 'open' textures as the melodic outline in octaves in the second piece, is little short of miraculous – nor surely can anyone have teased out so many inner lines in the Schubert/Godowsky *Moment musical* or with such delicious insouciance?

And what of his volcanic conception of the F minor *Ballade* – his scarcely less explosive reading of the Stojowski *Caprice orientale* explores a dynamic range that calls to mind Nyiregyházi's colossal inflation of Bortkiewicz's miniature *Travel Pictures*? True, many of the composer's dynamic indications are swept aside by the torrential force of the playing; true, not only is there a profusion of textual changes and amplified harmonic registrations, but also extended figurations which run the risk of disturbing the proportionality of the musical phraseology. But, equally, the metastructural balance he achieves between what Jim Samson describes as harmonically enclosed antecedents and progressive consequents is carried through with a compelling logic and an inexorable physical momentum which allow variation and transformation to unfold without a descent into mere episodic repetitiousness.

To Hofmann projection was paramount. To fail in this area was a discourtesy tantamount to whispering secrets in a crowded room. By the same token, rhythm represented order. It was, however, an inherently flexible rhythm, sustained by a temporal premise, whose underlying strength could accommodate the utmost interpretative fluidity without a weakening of its pivotal function. Such a strength did not preclude the viability of contrasting visions of the same material, as, for example, in the myriad subtle inflexions in his various readings of the first movement of the *Moonlight* Sonata, since it incorporated an organic expressive vocabulary rather than being affected by one imposed from outside. Given Hofmann's legendary near-infallibility, there are, surprisingly, a good many instances where accuracy appears to have been sacrificed to the communication of the music's turbulent inner life. Any suspicion, however, that Hofmann's technical powers were in serious decline at this stage in his career may be dismissed after listening to his breathtaking double-note wizardry in the reprise of his own

version of Chopin's *Minute Waltz*, which he dispatches with a throwaway nonchalance that leaves such pyrotechnicians as Michałowski, Zurawlew, Goldsand and Rosen on the starting blocks. Hofmann's ongoing search for integrated solutions to artistic problems was part of a larger quest towards a greater understanding of life itself through Art, in which every solution along the way radiated outward from a more vital realization of musical insights. Ironically, he saw boundaries, especially those self-imposed out of a deep respect for the creative genius of composers such as Beethoven, Schumann and Chopin, as drawn to secure the widest possible freedom. Yet he always remained true to Goethe's axiom: Outwardly confined. Inwardly boundless. **Charles Hopkins**

. . . .

Piano Recital Konstantin Lifschitz (pf). Palexa Ⓕ Ⓓ CD0507/8 (two discs: 121 minutes: DDD). Recorded at a performance in the Salle Pierre-Mercure, Centre Pierre-Péladeau, Montreal on November 24th, 1997.
Anonymous: Gagliarda Veneziana. **Chopin:** Mazurka in A flat, Op. 59 No. 2. **Haydn:** Piano Sonata No. 30 in D, HobXVI/19. **Mozart:** Romanze in A flat, KAnh205. Adagio in B minor, K540. March in C, K408 No. 1. Andante in F, K616. **Rameau:** Pièces de clavecin – Suite in E minor. **Schubert:** Impromptus, D899. Piano Sonata No. 20 in A, D959 – Andantino. **Scriabin:** Etude in B, Op. 8 No. 4.

Reviewing 21-year-old Konstantin Lifschitz's earlier Denon recordings (the first made when he was 13) of music ranging from Bach's *Goldberg Variations* to Ravel's *Gaspard de la nuit* I celebrated an imaginative vision, technical mastery and, dare I say it, a maturity far beyond his tender years. Since that time there have been disappointments (two nebulous, oddly uncommunicative recitals at London's Wigmore Hall) and so it is deeply gratifying to find this remarkable young Russian pianist, returning us, on this two-disc Montreal début album, to his finest form. Essentially 'low in tone', his concert eschews all obvious or popular appeal, ignoring delectable charmers or show-pieces in favour of introspection and some daringly chosen byways of the repertoire. In Schubert's *Impromptus*,

D899 he quietly points to details often obscured by other more celebrated and self-serving players. Such understatement means that he refuses to step out into the light in the heart's-easing second subject of the First *Impromptu*, avoids a hint of display in the Second *Impromptu*'s waltz-caprice cascades and confides the 'heavenly lengths' of the Third with rare distinction. Time and again (even when he so daringly eases his way into the A flat *Impromptu*'s central key-change, its clouding of former radiance, with little or no change of tempo) he follows the composer's innermost contour and vision with simple, unaffected and unforced artistry.

Elsewhere, his Mozart (a defining selection rather than the brilliance of one of the more bustling virtuoso sonatas) is no less telling, with every detail of the desolating B minor *Adagio* quietly but unmistakably registered. In Rameau and Haydn Lifschitz occasionally crosses the divide between understatement and diffidence (the Haydn surely needs a greater sense of projection to sustain its length: 16'20" with repeats in this performance as opposed to Pogorelich's more vivid and incisive reading lasting 11'49" – DG ① 435 618-2GH, 5/92), yet even here you are clearly listening to a master musician, one who draws you into a shadowland of subdued poetic beauty. The successful recordings point out that 'the dynamic range is that used by the musician' (a sinister reminder of the sort of trickery that goes on in some recording studios), the Montreal audience cheers its most unusual musical hero to the rafters and the entire recital is dedicated by Konstantin Lifschitz 'to my dear wife Galinka'. **Bryce Morrison**

....

Tiegerman – The Lost Legend of Cairo

[a]**Ignace Tiegerman** (pf); [b]**Henri Barda** (pf); [c]**Cairo Symphony Orchestra** / [d]**José Ferriz,** [e]**Oreste Campisi.**
Arbiter mono/[b]stereo Ⓟ ① ARBITER116 (two discs: 157 minutes; ADD). Also contains Theodor Leschetizky reciting his artistic credo (recorded on a cylinder in Vienna on January 17th, 1907) and Ignace Tiegerman speaking in Cairo (date unknown).
Brahms: Capriccio in B minor, Op. 76 No. 2[a]. Intermezzo in B flat minor, Op. 117 No. 2[a] (both recorded in Italy, c1965).

Romance in F, Op. 118 No. 5 (Cairo, c1955-7)[a]. Concerto for Piano and Orchestra No. 2 in B flat, Op. 83[ace] – Allegro non troppo; Allegro appassionato (broadcast performance, Cairo, May 18th, 1954). **Chopin**[a]: Ballade No. 4 in F minor, Op. 52. Barcarolle in F sharp, Op. 60. Etudes – A flat, Op. 10 No. 10; G sharp minor, Op. 25 No. 6. Nocturne No. 3 in B, Op. 9 No. 3. Preludes, Op. 28 – No. 7 in A; No. 8 in F sharp minor. Scherzo No. 1 in B minor, Op. 20 (all Cairo, mid-1950s). Piano Sonata No. 3 in B minor, Op. 58 (Radio Cairo, c1952). **Fauré:** Nocturne No. 4 in E flat, Op. 36 (Cairo, c1957-8)[a]. **Field:** Nocturnes[a] – No. 1 in E flat, H24; D minor, H59 (both Italy, c1965). **Franck:** Symphonic Variations[acd]. **Saint-Saëns:** Concerto for Piano and Orchestra No. 5 in F, 'Egyptian', Op. 103[acd] (both recorded at a performance in Cairo, June 1st, 1963). **Tiegerman:** Meditation[b] (New York, December 25th, 1998).

A chance remark by the daughter of Ignaz Friedman concerning a pianist named Ignace Tiegerman led producer Allan Evans on a voyage of discovery which he describes on page 54. To learn of an important pupil of Leschetizky who has been forgotten is curious, but to then be able to trace private recordings to substantiate the talent is extraordinary.

The great pianists of the past are represented today primarily by their recordings and, to a lesser extent, by reports of their concerts. If Rosenthal, d'Albert, Busoni and Godowsky had not been enticed into the recording studio we would have little actual idea of their work. Of course, today these records have come to represent these artists and it is unfair to judge them exclusively on such evidence; Godowsky and Busoni hated recording and Busoni's discs hardly reveal a pianist of the talents we read of. The contemporaries who left no recordings today seem less conspicuous. Joseffy and Stavenhagen, pupils of Liszt who lived long enough to have made records but didn't, are now merely names in books, while Ignace Tiegerman (1893-1968), who apparently made no commercial recordings, has been almost entirely forgotten.

The recordings presented here date from when Tiegerman was living in Cairo; they were all privately made, either captured live or taken from radio broadcasts, and the age of the tapes, coupled with their fragility and storage in an unsuitable climate, results in sound of variable quality. Fortunately, around 1965, the conductor Oreste Campisi took Tiegerman into a studio in Italy where he recorded a few short pieces. These particular recordings, which open each CD, are in excellent sound and display facets found in the playing of many Leschetizky pupils, particularly the warm tone and beautiful phrasing heard in both the Field and Brahms pieces.

The majority of the performances come from two sources. The recording of the farewell recital of 1963 in which he plays Franck and Saint-Saëns with a rather poor orchestra, is in good sound and the vivacity of the playing, particularly in the *Egyptian* Concerto, belies the fact that Tiegerman was 70 at the time. The sound quality in a run-through of a Chopin recital recorded by a pupil in the mid-1950s is far from satisfactory, but despite this one should not complain; the performances certainly *are* good. In fact, the playing of the larger Chopin works reminds one of Friedman in its sweep and grandeur, its passion and romanticism, and the B major *Nocturne* from Op. 9 is given a performance of great depth and beauty.

The two Chopin *Etudes* are in better sound and the pupil with the tape recorder is heard to suggest that Tiegerman play the *Etude* in thirds (Op. 25 No. 6). 'Ah, les doubles tierces!', he replies and plunges straight into it, even doubling the downward scale near the end as Friedman does on his recording (Pearl ⅅ IF2000, 12/90 or APR ⅅ APR7014, 1/93). The B minor Sonata, taken from a broadcast, is a performance painted on a broad canvas and it is interesting to compare it with a modern recording by a Tiegerman pupil, Henri Barda (Calliope ⅅ CAL6680). The opening in both recordings has an air of authority and declamation, a stage presence that demands attention. Both pianists also take the slow movement at a slightly faster pace than usual. The sound here is problematic, but when one's ears become accustomed to it, the rewards of the performance repay the effort.

The two movements from the Brahms B flat major Concerto demonstrate some of the 'emotional violence' that was noted by critics

in the 1920s. It is a volcanic performance where Tiegerman and the orchestra heroically soar aloft. This is the earliest of the recordings and here the sound is harsh but clear and I am told it will be better when released than on my review copy.

This issue is not for the faint of heart nor those whose prime concern is sound quality. What we have here is a historical document of the utmost importance that represents a major pianist of the Leschetizky school whose talent and identity, but for the rescue of these important recordings, would have been lost for ever.

Jonathan Summers

....

Great Pianists of the 20th Century – John Ogdon .John Ogdon (pf).

Philips Great Pianists of the 20th Century
Ⓜ ⅅ 456 913-2PM2 (two discs: 154 minutes: ADD). Released in association with Steinway & Sons.
Alkan: Etudes dans les tons mineurs, Op. 39 – Concerto (RCA USA LSC3192).
Busoni: Nine Variations on Chopin's C minor Prelude, K213*a* (HMV ASD434, 8/61). Concerto for Piano and Orchestra, K247 (John Alldis Choir; Royal Philharmonic Orchestra / Daniel Revenaugh. HMV ASD2336/7, 1/68).
Rachmaninov: Piano Sonata No. 2 in B flat minor, Op. 36 (from RCA SB6793, 8/69).
Scriabin: Piano Sonata No. 4 in F sharp, Op. 30 (HMV SLS814, 11/71).

At his final Queen Elizabeth Hall recital in 1989, John Ogdon played a first half of dismaying awfulness – the Chopin, Balakirev and Brahms at times unrecognizable beneath the clouds of lithium-induced confusion – before producing Liszt playing in the second which was at least as great as anything I had ever heard. A week later he was dead, leaving us with the memories of a recital which seemed in retrospect to have been a distillation of the vicissitudes of his performing career – the highs and lows perhaps starker than ever before. Nobody who heard Ogdon live on one of his better days would dispute his place amongst the great pianists of the century, yet many of his recordings document the same inconsistencies as his live performances. Indeed, someone hearing Ogdon for the first time via this first of Philips's two sets might wonder whether 'great pianists' are permitted so often to leave details sketched in, or to fumble articulation as concentration falters. If Ogdon often lacked constancy and finish, however, his panoramic vision could reveal important new vistas and, whilst his orchestral sonority matched his huge physical girth, his melting tenderness quite belied it.

Philips could have chosen more imaginatively in presenting Ogdon on more consistently inspired form – he was marvellous in Debussy, for example, and yet recorded very little, but his three *Etudes* from the Melodiya LP (⊙ D10515/16), two *Préludes* and 'Clair de lune' from the early EMI recital (⊙ ALP1995, 10/63) would have been particularly welcome. As it is, Philips has opted for the kind of large-scale high romantic works with which Ogdon was popularly associated; even then, the selections are sometimes misplaced. Rachmaninov's Second Sonata (sadly in the gouged-out revised version) shows a real sensitivity to the composer's rich sound world and yet a number of choppy passages suggest repertoire hastily prepared – the First Sonata, with which this was coupled on the original RCA LP (⊙ SB6793, 8/69), was the far superior performance. Similarly the Fourth was never Ogdon's most successful Scriabin sonata in concert and neither was it a highlight of his EMI integral set (① CZS5 72652-2, 11/71^R); although there are some engrossing passages early on, a feeling of brusque routine permeates many bars and the final section is too scrappy to generate any real sense of fervour or impact. The Alkan Concerto also has its fair share of lapses – most notably in the often slipshod last movement – and the recorded sound is horribly tainted by peak distortion (deriving from RCA's original masters) but, in spite of the unevenness, the inspiration often runs high and the overview is thrilling; I could think of no better recording to play to demonstrate that the Concerto was the work of an exotic quasi-genius rather than an eccentric note-spinning recluse (as it so often sounds).

The second disc of works by Busoni finds Ogdon on firmer ground, his attention unwavering and his focus resolute. The recording of the *Variations on Chopin's C minor Prelude* was set down in the pianist's first studio sessions and demonstrates a tight grasp of the work's central thread. The Concerto, recorded in 1967 and in and out of the catalogue ever since, hardly needs an introduction. Others may since have performed the work with greater attention to Busoni's idiom, but the Ogdon recording is marked by a palpable sense of occasion and undoubtedly played a major part in reviving the work's fortunes. Nevertheless, with the Concerto having received wide currency over the years, the magnificent *Fantasia contrappuntistica* recording Ogdon made for Altarus – either the 1985 reading previously issued (⊙ AIR-2-9074) or the 1986 second take not yet released but said to be greater still – could have been the more perceptive choice. **Michael Glover**

....

Piano Recital Aleksandar Serdar (pf). EMI Debut ⑧ ① CDZ5 72821-2 (74 minutes: DDD). **Bach/Busoni:** Chaconne in D minor. **Brahms:** 16 Waltzes, Op. 39. **Chopin:** Andante spianato and Grande Polonaise in E flat, Op. 22. **Galuppi:** Piano Sonata No. 5 in C. **Mendelssohn:** Variations sérieuses in D minor, Op. 54.

Beethoven Piano Sonata No. 28 in A, Op. 101. **Brahms** 25 Variations and Fugue on a Theme by G. F. Handel, Op. 24. **Mozart** Piano Sonata No. 18 in D, K576. **Jonathan Gilad** (pf). EMI Debut ⑧ ① CDZ5 72823-2 (64 minutes: DDD).

Piano Recital Haesun Paik (pf). EMI Debut ⑧ ① CDZ5 72827-2 (60 minutes: DDD). **Mendelssohn:** Songs without Words – Allegretto in F sharp minor, Op. 30 No. 6; Andante con moto in A flat, Op. 53 No. 1; Andante grazioso in A, Op. 62 No. 6; Presto in C, Op. 67 No. 4. **Mozart:** Fantasia in D minor, K397/K385g. **Ravel:** La valse (arr. cpsr and Paik). **Schumann:** Humoreske in B flat, Op. 20. Kinderszenen, Op. 15 – Träumerei.

Since EMI's Debut series serves to champion musicians 'on the brink of major careers,' you might well approach these discs expecting a high level of self-promotion in the form of technical display and interpretative posturing. In fact, these three recitals are united not by any bursts of flamboyance, but rather by their unpretentiousness, their refusal to impose on either the music or the listener. At first, this modesty is a welcome surprise, but in the long run it turns out to be a qualified virtue.

Certainly, Belgrade-born Aleksander Serdar wins plaudits for his non-percussive touch (most evident in his gracious *legato* and his eagerness to explore the quiet end of the dynamic spectrum), his limpid textures (say, in the fourth of the Mendelssohn *Variations sérieuses*) and his silky passagework. His recital gets off to a breathtaking start with a luminous reading of the Galuppi Fifth Sonata, spun out with such pure tone, such fluidity of phrasing and such delicate filigree that it rivals even Michelangeli's famous Decca account (① 417 772-2DM, 11/89). His secretive, moonlit *Andante spianato* is similarly seductive, as are the more confidential of the Mendelssohn Variations and the Brahms *Waltzes*.

I don't want to suggest that Serdar's playing is uniformly unassertive: certainly, his dance through Brahms's Sixth *Waltz* deftly catches the spirit of the quirky rhythms. But his performances could fairly be described as genteel, and his cultivation sometimes gets in the way of the music. He's not especially sympathetic, for instance, to the paprika of the 11th *Waltz*; and while he's surely capable of stern expression and solid sound (say, in the beginning of the Bach/Busoni), he rarely calls on his reserves of strength and even more rarely tightens the springs on his rhythms. The Mendelssohn and Brahms have enough richness of detail to withstand this kind of subtle examination, even though their momentum is sometimes compromised. But the *Polonaise* section of the Chopin diptych is not one of the composer's deepest creations, and it firmly resists such coaxing – indeed, stripped of the bravura that is its primary reason for being, it sounds oddly plain, even pointless. And given Serdar's interpretative temperance, it seems a miscalculation for him to have taken on Busoni's most monumental revisiting of Bach, rather than some less flamboyant Bach original.

The suitability of performing style to repertoire is similarly inconsistent in Jonathan Gilad's recital, recorded when the precocious French pianist was just 16. On the positive side, his finely wrought Mozart reveals an almost miraculous range of *sotto voce* tonal resources.

True, especially when heard in the context of Fazil Say's more buoyant and more sharply profiled Mozart début album (Warner Music ① 3984-21970-2, 9/98), Gilad could reasonably be accused of understatement (he steals through the second movement at nearly a whisper). Still, the performance is so beguiling that it's churlish to complain.

But the craggier idiom of late Beethoven doesn't respond as gratefully to Gilad's lapidary artistry. Here, neither his scrupulous care over details of articulation nor his pristine balances in the music's more complex textures can quite compensate for his lack of forward pressure, much less his unwillingness to engage the music's dramatic conflicts. The Brahms, for all its exquisite moments (the deft inner voices in the Second Variation, the feathery touch in the 16th), seems too manicured and deferential as well.

The most flashy playing on these three discs comes in Haesun Paik's account of her own amplification of Ravel's already-virtuosic transcription of *La valse*. But she, too, steers clear of exhibitionism elsewhere. The restraint pays off in her intimate performance of Mendelssohn's 'Venezianisches Gondellied' (Op. 30 No. 6) and the dreamier passages in the Schumann *Humoreske* (for instance, the gentle opening). But it provides less consistent dividends in her Mozart, where she discounts the music's initial tensions; and it misfires even more seriously in the more febrile episodes of the Schumann, where, for all her technical aplomb, her unswerving commitment to decorum subverts the impertinent contrast that lies at the heart of Schumann's contestatory style. And even the Ravel, for all its smouldering power, sometimes turns muddy as thick textures smother the main material.

Certainly, nothing on Paik's disc generates the kind of electricity heard in her Tchaikovsky Piano Concerto (CPI ① 329405), much less the Scriabin Fifth Sonata (Tonmeister Recordings ① UMKAPELL89) recorded – although not widely distributed – a decade ago in the wake of her victory in the 1989 Kapell Competition. And listening to her rather cramped playing in the context of the other two discs does prompt some uneasy speculations. Is it possible that the very opportunity to participate in a distinct 'debut' series – one that offers a single-disc exposure on one of the major labels – so discourages playfulness and risk-taking that strength of personality gets sapped? Whatever the cause, what we have here are three unquestionably talented young pianists giving thoughtful but rarely venturesome performances of largely mainstream repertoire that has already received countless recordings of greater individuality. At EMI's bargain price, it's still worth giving these CDs your attention – just don't expect any shocks along the lines of those provided by the discs that have recently introduced us to Konstantin Lifschitz (Denon ① CO-78907, 12/94), Arcadi Volodos (Sony Classical ① SK62691, A/97), Tian Ying (Arizona Friends of Chamber Music, unnumbered), or Fazil Say. The notes are on the brief side, but except for some extraneous sounds that intrude on Gilad's playing, the engineering is first-rate. **Peter J. Rabinowitz**

....

Great Pianists of the 20th Century – Alexis Weissenberg Alexis Weissenberg (pf).

Philips Great Pianists of the 20th Century dhmono/stereo Ⓜ ① 456 988-2PM2 (two discs: 155 minutes: ADD/efgDDD). Item marked a from La voix de son maître 2C 167 11123/5 (recorded 1965/7), bHMV ASD2971 (6/72), cHMV SLS838 (5/73), dLumen LD3-400 (1955), eDG 427 499-2GH (4/90), fDG 415 510-1GH (6/86), g415 511-2GH (6/86), hAmerican Columbia ML2099 (1950), iRCA DPS2020 (6/72), jLa voix de son maître ASDF902 (1964). Released in association with Steinway & Sons.
Bach: Partita No. 4 in D, BWV828a. Prelude in B minor, BWV855a (arr. Siloti)b. **Chopin:** Nocturnesc – No. 17 in B, Op. 62 No. 1; No. 18 in E, Op. 62 No. 2. **Czerny:** Five Variations on a theme of Rode, Op. 33d. **Debussy:** Estampesf. **Bach/Liszt:** Prelude and Fugue in A minor, S462b. **Prokofiev:** Piano Sonata No. 3 in A minor, Op. 28h. Suggestion diabolique, 'Temptation', Op. 4 No. 4h. **Rachmaninov:** Prelude in B minor, Op. 32 No. 10i. Piano Sonata No. 1 in D minor, Op. 28e. **D. Scarlatti:** Keyboard Sonatasg – B minor, Kk87; F, Kk107; A minor, Kk109; F minor, Kk184. **Scriabin:** Etude No. 11 in B flat minor, Op. 8h. Nocturne for the left hand, Op. 9h. **Stravinsky:** Petrushka – three movementsj.

Weissenberg's unique pianism has always been a difficult topic to assess, given the controversy inevitably generated by his performances, whether live or on disc. In Britain the critical reception has generally ranged from cool to hostile, while in certain other countries he is held in the highest esteem. Although Weissenberg has been mostly inactive during the last few years, this compilation from Philips may prompt a fresh look at those qualities that clearly distinguish him from his colleagues.

It is gratifying to note that Philips has managed to reissue Weissenberg's very first recording, a ten-inch LP for American Columbia dating from 1950, made when the pianist was just 21. The two Prokofiev works from that disc already reveal the powerful technique, the headlong rhythmic drive, the highly individual use of rubato and the almost defiant conviction that underlie his musical thinking. An unmistakable vein of poetry and sensitivity is evident, too, in the Scriabin *Nocturne* and *Etude*. From five years later come the Czerny *Variations on a theme of Rode*, Op. 33, a work that was brought to Weissenberg's attention through Horowitz's incomparable 1944 recording for RCA Victor (① GD60451, 11/91). Weissenberg matches the elegant exuberance and lapidarian tonal polish of Horowitz while adding a definite flair of his own.

The Bach *Partita* in D major has been a staple of Weissenberg's recitals for many years. This performance comes from his set of the complete *Partitas*, recorded in France during the 1960s. His jet-propelled tempos in the faster sections, combined with little or no dynamic shading, sometimes produce the effect of notes breathlessly tumbling over one another, yet there is a brio and vitality here, all kept under iron control, that is contagious. Much the same applies to the Scarlatti pieces from Weissenberg's more recent DG collection.

With the Rachmaninov Sonata No. 1 and the Stravinsky *Petrushka* scenes we find the pianist at his most aggressive, producing interpretations that are stunning in their impact, relentless in their forward sweep, breathtaking and exhausting to behold. The sheer audacity of Weissenberg's approach, and the unfaltering resources he draws upon in the process, usually make any protests purely academic. Yet this is not the kind of playing that could ever be called ingratiating, and the final impression tends to be one of awe rather than love for what Weissenberg has accomplished. Some will find it irresistible, others repellent; but as has been said before, this is piano playing on a level that simply cannot be ignored.

In terms of repertoire these discs offer an acceptable cross-section of the music Weissenberg has favoured, although personally I would have included examples of his Haydn and Schumann interpretations as well. Sonically the restorations wear their years lightly except for the rather fuzzy Czerny, which has obviously been transferred from a less-than-pristine copy of the original (now quite rare) Lumen LP and then subjected to some heavy-handed processing. Was Philips unable to obtain the mastertape? If so, a word of explanation would have been welcome. **Donald Manildi**

....

Eileen Joyce Parlophone Recordings, 1933-40. **Eileen Joyce** (pf).
Testament mono Ⓟ Ⓒ SBT1174 (77 minutes: ADD).
d'Albert: Scherzo, Op. 16 No. 2 (from Parlophone E11391, 3/39). **Bach:** Prelude and Fugue in A minor, BWV944 (E11354, 4/38). **S. Bergman:** Polka Caprice, Op. 1 No. 3. Himmelgesang, Op. 2 No. 1 (both from E11363, 7/38). **Debussy:** Pour le piano – Toccata (E11239, 12/33). **Dohnányi:** Rhapsody in C, Op. 11 No. 3 (E11351, 3/38). **Fauré:** Impromptu No. 2 in F minor, Op. 31 (E11372, 10/38). **Grieg:** Scherzo-impromptu, Op. 73 No. 3 (E11427, 1/40). Lyric Pieces, Op. 43 – No. 1, Butterfly; No. 2, Lonely wanderer (both E11411, 6/39); No. 6, To the Spring (E11427, 1/40); Melody, Op. 47 No. 3; Brooklet, Op. 62 No. 4 (both E11411, 6/39). Summer's eve, Op. 71 No. 2 (E11427). **Liszt:** La leggierezza, S144 No. 2 (E11237, 9/33). Gnomenreigen, S145 No. 2 (R1965, 12/34). **Moszkowski:** Valse in E, Op. 34 No. 1 (E11239, 12/33). **Palmgren:** En route, Op. 9 (E11246, 4/34). **Paradis:** Toccata in A (E11354, 4/38). **Rachmaninov:** Preludes – G minor, Op. 23 No. 5 (E11252, 6/34); A flat, Op. 23 No. 8; A minor, Op. 32 No. 8 (both E11377, 11/38). **Schlözer:** Etude in A flat, Op. 1 No. 2 (E11237, 9/33). **C. Scott:** Lotus Land, Op. 47 No. 1. Danse nègre, Op. 58 No. 3 (both E11333, 10/37). **Sinding:** Rustle of Spring, Op. 32

No. 3 (E11427, 1/40). **R. Strauss** (arr. Gieseking): Ständchen, Op. 17 No. 2 (recorded 1965).

Although Eileen Joyce was younger than Horowitz and only three years older than Earl Wild, her active career was so short that she seems to belong to a more distant generation – an impression only magnified by some of the old-fashioned selections on this recital. But if both her reputation and the repertoire are slightly faded, her playing assuredly is not. Fellow *IPQ* contributor Bryce Morrison (who contributes a personal reminiscence on page 34) was a friend of Joyce's towards the end of her life and chose the recordings for the disc; his selection of performances that emphasize the 'short, witty, dazzling and incisive' shows her off as a pianist of uncommon brilliance.

I use the word 'brilliance' advisedly, to point to both the virtues and the drawbacks of the recital. On the positive side, these up-tempo readings are uniformly thrilling, as Joyce tosses off the most rapid and intricate filigree with unassuming agility. Few other pianists have articulated Liszt's *La leggierezza* with such glittering facility, for instance, and fewer still have so sharply detailed the mercurial flight patterns of Grieg's *Butterfly*. But she does purchase her spark at a price. In part because of her treble-tilted sonority, and in part because she's better at negotiating rapid runs than at balancing chords, her playing often lacks weight; and because dry tone and brittle touch often thwart a true *legato*, melodies rarely blossom under her fingers. No wonder, then, that she's more alert to the busy ornamentation than to the vocal line in the Strauss/Gieseking *Ständchen*, or that her extravagance of detail obscures the melodic shape of Rachmaninov's *Prelude*, Op. 23 No. 8, or that when performing Dohnányi's Prokofiev-meets-Brahms C major *Rhapsody*, she's more persuasive in the skittish diablerie than in the reflective passages that intervene.

Still, whatever the limitations of Joyce's art, the dash of this recital is infectious – and the transfers are up to Testament's usual high standards. The overlap with Pearl's Joyce pot-pourri (Ⓒ GEMMCD9022) is unfortunate; but it is sufficiently small (six items) for this new disc to be warmly recommended to fanciers of keyboard pyrotechnics. **Peter J. Rabinowitz**

IPQ SUBSCRIPTION ORDER FORM

By subscribing to **IPQ** you will save more than 10% on four times the cover price and protect yourself against future price increases. You will also have your copies delivered to your door before the magazine is available in the shops.

International Piano Quarterly is published four times a year: in Spring (April), Summer (July), Autumn (October) and Winter (January). **IPQ** is available worldwide by postal subscription.

This form can be used to pay for subscriptions and single copies of **IPQ** as well as Classified advertisements.

Subscriptions

	Annual subscription	Delivery
☐ Great Britain	£16·00	3-4 days
☐ Europe	£20·00	7-14 days
☐ North America	US $38·00	7-21 days
☐ Rest of the World	£22·00	7-21 days

☐ Please enter my subscription to **IPQ** commencing with the issue dated:

Back issues
☐ Great Britain   £4·50
☐ Europe   £5·50
☐ North America   US $10·00
☐ Rest of the World   £6·50

Please send me the following issue(s)
☐ Spring 1998   ☐ Winter 1998
☐ Autumn 1998

☐ Classified advertisement Payment

Name

Address

Post/Zip code

Payment
Payment can be made by (please tick appropriate box)
☐ Cheque
☐ Sterling bank draft
☐ International Money Order
☐ British Postal Order
☐ Eurocheque
☐ Credit Card (see below)

Payment being made in sterling (or US$ if resident in the USA)

Subscription   = £

Single copy   = £

Classified advertisement   = £

Total   . = £

PAYMENT BY CREDIT CARD

Please charge my:
Visa/Trustcard/Barclaycard
(Charge can be in US $ if resident in the USA)

Mastercard/Eurocard
Switch - Issue no

Card number

Expiry date

Name and address on credit card if different from above

Signature

Name

Address

Post/Zip code

Please make cheques payable to Gramophone Publications Limited and send this form to:
Gramophone, 135 Greenford Road, Sudbury Hill, Harrow, Middlesex HA1 3YD, Great Britain
Telephone +44 (0)181-422 4562 **Fax** +44 (0)181-869 8404

IPQ CLASSIFIED ADVERTISEMENTS

To advertise

Telephone +44(0)181-422 4562 **Fax** +44(0)181-869 8402

Copy and remittance for Summer 1999 should be received by May 26th, 1999. If received too late it will be included in the Autumn 1999 issue unless we are advised to the contrary.

Advertisements can be placed over the telephone or fax with the **IPQ** classified department on the above number or by post to Jo Frost, **IPQ** Classified, 135 Greenford Road, Sudbury Hill, Harrow, Middlesex HA1 3YD, Great Britain.

Rates UK and EC countries Linage is 53p per word for a single insertion, 51p per word for insertions in two or three issues and 47p per word in four or more issues.

Semi-display is costed per centimetre (approx ⅜ inch) £16·45 for a single insertion, £15·63 for insertions appearing in two or three issues and £14·81 in four or more issues.

Value Added Tax is included in the above figures.

Rates Overseas excluding EC (US$ in brackets) Linage is 45p (US$0·79) per word for a single insertion, 43p (US$0·75) per word for insertions in two or three issues and 40p (US$0·70) per word in four or more issues.

Semi-display is costed per centimetre (approximately ⅜ inch) £14·00 (US$15·75) for a single insertion, £13·30 (US$14·96) for insertions in two or three issues and £12·60 (US$14·17) in four or more issues.

Typesetting charges are made for semi-display advertisements, advised on receipt of copy.

Box numbers £2·30 extra ($4·03 for USA). Replies should be sent to "Box No..." c/o **IPQ**, 135 Greenford Road, Sudbury Hill, Harrow, Middlesex HA1 3YD, Great Britain.

Please note that the name, address and/or telephone number in the advertisement must be paid for.

Telephone numbers count as two words. E-mail and website addresses count as three words.

Payment must be sent with advertisement copy or the advertisement will not appear.

Cheques and Postal Orders should be made payable to Gramophone Publications Limited.

Payment can be made by Access credit card or Barclaycard. Please use the form on page 108 and send it with your advertisement copy.

Trade Descriptions Act The publishers retain the right to refuse or withdraw advertisements at their discretion and accept no responsibility for matters arising from clerical or printers' errors or of an advertiser not completing his contract.

Advertisements are carried on the assumption that they comply with the provisions of the Trade Descriptions Act 1968, the British Code of Advertising and the Mechanical Copyright Protection Society Limited.

Under the Business Advertisements (Disclosure) Order 1977 it is an offence for anyone advertising in the course of their business to pass the advertisement off as being that of a private individual.

Records for sale

UK readers are reminded that both VAT and Import Duty may be payable on recordings purchased outside the EC

AMERICA'S LARGEST NEW/USED/COLLECTOR SHOP
•TOP DOLLAR PAID FOR COLLECTIONS•
150,000 Titles: 40,000 Classical LPs • 10,000 Classical CDs
Also Jazz, Rock etc   *We buy and sell*

PRINCETON RECORD EXCHANGE
TEL: (609) 921-0881 Web# http:www.prex.com
20 TULANE ST., PRINCETON, NJ 08542, USA
Easy Access from NYC – Call or Write for Free Brochure

FOR THE SERIOUS MUSIC LOVER

Fine Classical LPs, Condition Guaranteed

♪ specialist in audiophile and collector LPs, mono and stereo, also great pianists

♪ set sale lists are published bi-monthly, free to collectors (or just music lovers), very competitive pricing with guaranteed grading

Write, phone or fax:

STEVEN L. WILLNER

🎼 *Fine Classical Records*

14720 Harvest Lane
Silver Spring, MD 20905 U.S.A.
Telephone: 301-236-0375
Fax: 301-879-1433

COLLECTION DUMAZERT
54 Rue Blanche 75009 PARIS
Tel: 33 1 64 04 23 85 / Fax: 33 1 64 20 06 04

Regular free list by auction   **78RPM LP**
CLASSICAL, OPERA, VARIETIES   More than 300,000 items
Email: rpm78@club-internet.fr

WING RECORDS
'SIC TRANSIT GLORIA MUNDI'

Regular lists of Classical LPs: historical, audiophile, books, programs, photos, sale list. Watch for our up-coming Web-site

Charles B Jones, P.O. Box 196, Cheshire, Ct. 06410
USA, Tel & Fax: 203 271 0073

NORBECK & PETERS
Elusive Historical CDs: Marston, Preiser, Romophone, IRCC, TIMAClub, VRCS, Walhall, Clama, Delos, Myto, Fonovox, Claremont, Blue Moon, Aria, The Record Collector, etc.
Books by & about musicians. Yearly auctions of Rarer Vocal & Instrumental LPs & 78s.
Ephemera & Autographed Photos.
Visa & Mastercard accepted. Same day service.
PO Box 4, Woodstock, NY 12498 USA.
TEL: (914) 679-6982. FAX: (914) 679-6904
e-mail: norpete@aol.com   web site: http://www.norpete.com

Great pianists and all fine quality classical LPs. Detailed catalogue from Spiral Classics. Tel: (+44) 01509 557846 or fax: (+44) 01509 557847 (Britain)

Rare piano LPs (Feinberg, Ginsburg, Neuhaus, Nikolajeva, Sofronitsky, Vedernikov, Annie Fischer, Melodiya, Supraphon, Eterna, Hungaroton). Please call or write for free list. Discorara, Budapest 114, Pf 303, H-1536, Hungary. Tel/fax: (+36) 1 325 6753

PIANO RARITIES & SPECIAL ISSUES

ARRAU, BACKHAUS, DE LARA, GIESEKING, GOULD, GILELS, GINZBERG, INNA HEIFETZ, LAMOND, LORTAT, MICHELANGELI, MOISEIWITSCH, PETRI, PUGNO, PLANYE, RICHTER, RUBINSTEIN, ROSENTHAL, SAPELLNIKOV, SHEHORI, SCHNABEL, SAUER, PETRI, SOFRONITSKY, TURECK, YUDINA and many others,

Also a large selection on L.P.

Callers or by post (some lists available).

MICHAEL G. THOMAS

5A, Norfolk Place,
London W2 1QN
Tel (0171) 723 4935 *Monday – Friday*

THE RING MAIL ORDER SERVICE

Large selection of classical piano records and CDs available. Top quality and very reasonable prices.

Lists available for all categories of music.
Piano – orchestral – violin – military – jazz, etc.
Visa/Mastercard
PO Box 69, Saffron Walden CB11 3UT
Tel/Fax: 01799 543700
Evenings & Weekends: 01799 540843
www.ringmail.com Email: enquiries@ringmail.com

Piano scores wanted: Friedman, Godowsky, Grainger, Henselt, Medtner, Thalberg. Box No. 8971 (Surrey) c/o IPQ

The Collection of The Classical Pianist is available to all. Live performances, telecasts and more - pianists only. Free supplements. P.O. Box 485, Gurnee, IL 60031-0485 USA

Books

Looking for an out-of print book? Let me find it for you
All subjects   No search fee   No commitment to buy
John Dwyer. Newgate Books, 3 Quatre Bras, Hexham, Northumberland, NE46 3JY   Tel/Fax: 01434 607650

SECONDHAND MUSIC BOOKS
SCORES & SHEET MUSIC
Our wide-ranging catalogues of 1000's of different titles are issued monthly.
DECORUM BOOKS (IPQ)
24 Cloudesley Square London N1 0HN
Tel 0171 278 1838   Fax 0171 837 6424

Societies

'Cziffra - live in Argentina' CDs here soon. Contact Cziffra Society, 19 Ragsdale Street, Rothwell, Northants NN14 6DE. Tel: (+44) 01536 710 375

IPQ INDEX TO ADVERTISERS

When live doesn't mean live

PIANO RECORDINGS are often said to be the hardest to edit – more so than orchestral or vocal – on account of pedalling and voicing being so tricky to match across splices. Nevertheless, the difficulties do not prevent many producers from piecing together recordings that are mosaics of tiny patches, creating recorded 'performances' that could never have existed in the concert hall. Modern digital editing systems have made the process easier to manage and, given the amount of work that can now be accomplished speedily via artful clicks of a computer mouse, cheaper than ever before. Should listeners be alarmed by such high-tech alchemy; should CDs carry tags akin to the ingredients listings on processed food, stating how many takes and how many edits went into the finished product?

Whilst no one can deny that pianists and producers are consenting adults, free to press whatever buttons they please within the privacy of their studios, a growing number of artists are using the capabilities of modern technology as a substitute for properly preparing repertoire. Instances of pianists virtually sight-reading material in the studio and then failing disastrously when invited to repeat the performance in public are becoming increasingly common. Clearly, recordings do still carry with them an implication that they genuinely reflect the artist's level of accomplishment, albeit with clinkers removed – why else would there be so many surprised expressions when a pianist falls flat on his face trying to match even approximately the entirely artificial fluency of a recent recording? Such artistic disingenuousness should not be confused with the school of multi-take recording which approaches the task of committing a performance to disc as a fundamentally different process from seeking to capture a live performance. A number of today's pianists have produced satisfying recordings that have been assembled from copious takes, each take selected on the basis of optimal fit into the overall musical thread. Such an approach, using liberal amounts of tape not to camouflage technical inadequacy but to produce an idealized 'studio interpretation', might be regarded as harnessing modern technology to hone musical creativity – just so long as the results are not held up as a benchmark for live performance, but are heard in a different context. Indeed, such a method has interesting parallels with the approach to performance revealed in Pierre-Martin Juban's article on Sofronitsky (A/98), where the pianist was reported as having numerous interpretations of each passage, spontaneously choosing between them as he played.

No such justification can be offered for the 'live recording' scam, however, where a disc is presented as a document of a live concert, whilst actually being riddled with edits and with not a disclaimer in sight. Strong concerns were voiced at the time CBS released its two-LP set of Horowitz's 1965 Carnegie Hall 'Historic Return' recital (or 'Hysterical Return', as Glenn Gould caustically referred to the event), after it transpired that patches had been used to cover serial mishaps in the second-movement coda of Schumann's *Fantasy*. Yet in spite of doctoring in the Schumann – Horowitz had claimed the mistakes in the coda had been an 'Act of God' caused by perspiration falling into his eyes – the abundant errors elsewhere went uncorrected. Three decades later the industry is far more cavalier still – several labels have issued high profile discs of 'live' concerts, some of which actually contain more material from audience-free patching sessions than from the live event. Editing out coughs and wrong notes may sometimes be commercially desirable (though personally I prefer to hear the original concert, warts and all), but alerting buyers that 'live' doesn't mean wholly live is, at the very least, a courtesy and is also, strictly speaking, a legal necessity. ^{IPQ} **Michael Glover**